Countdown to Christmas

Have a Very Merry Movie Holiday!

Caroline McKenzie

FOREWORD BY
Candace Cameron Bure

INTRODUCTION BY
Rachel Hardage Barrett

HEARST
HOME

CONTENTS

P eople often ask me what brings me back to Hallmark Channel holiday movies time and again. That's simple: It's Christmas! While the roles are delectably fun—I've time traveled, played my own twin sister, and nursed a reindeer back to health—the real joy comes from reveling in the holidays.

I'm someone who puts my tree up the day after Thanksgiving (stopping to recall the significance of each ornament), bakes cookies for every teacher, neighbor, and mailman in my life (my mom's top-secret crispy chocolate chip recipe), and never fails to round up aunts, uncles, and cousins for caroling (we are a family of performers, and our rendition of "Go Tell It on the Mountain" is as exuberant as it gets).

That is all to say I wholeheartedly embrace the joy and unconditional love that personifies the meaning of Christmas. Which is why Hallmark films are so dear to me. No matter what time of year you're filming, when you step onto the set, the spirit of the season instantly invigorates. Snow is falling, Nat King Cole is singing, trees are gleaming, and Santa Claus may or may not be just around the corner—it is impossible not to have a smile on your face. Because even if it's July and you're sweating through your red peacoat, in that moment it is Christmastime. There's an undeniable happiness and generosity in the air. (I can attest that Hallmark's casts and crews are the kindest around!) My steps become lighter and my days brighter.

I hope this book, with its many recipes, crafts, and film spotlights, evokes that same feeling for you—allowing you to savor the magic and warmth of the most wonderful time of the year for just a bit longer. 'Tis the season to share the love!

—CANDACE CAMERON BURE

As the editor of *Country Living*, I have long been aware that Hallmark holiday movies have serious mass appeal. Our magazine's audience of 30-plus million can't get enough of them, and you can count me as one of the feel-good network's devotees.

In a world with so much uncertainty, it's reassuring to take heart in the fact that, by the time the credits roll, everything will be okay—the small-town bakery will be saved, the spirit of Christmas will prevail, the community will come together, and, yes (spoiler alert!), Candace Cameron Bure will find everlasting love with the handsome single dad in the puffy vest. Skeptics may "bah humbug" the predictability of these movies, but what they don't understand is that's the whole point. For many, the movies provide the perfect backdrop to their favorite holiday rituals, whether it's decorating the tree, baking cookies, or wrapping gifts. The movies' set designers go to great lengths to infuse every single shot with holiday spirit—lights! garland! ornaments!—and that attention to detail serves up joy in spades. And when the holidays already feel so fleeting, don't we want to maximize our jolly per second? The yuletide scenes also let us vicariously check

off a seasonal bucket list for those of us who may not have a chance to, say, chop down our own tree, enter the gingerbread house contest, or go ice skating, caroling, or wassailing (whatever that actually is). We can live out these traditions via the screen or be inspired to forge our own festive future. Yes, I should learn to ice sculpture. Maybe I will join the town choir.

If you're holding this book in your hands, chances are you've already consumed the Hallmark Channel eggnog (good for you!), but even if you haven't, these pages are sure to leave you feeling as cozy as a cable-knit Christmas sweater. The world throws us enough curveballs, and a Hallmark holiday movie—like a beautifully decorated bed-and-breakfast in small-town Vermont—offers warm and welcome refuge.

—**RACHEL HARDAGE BARRETT**
EDITOR, *COUNTRY LIVING*

CHAPTER 1

SETTING THE SCENE

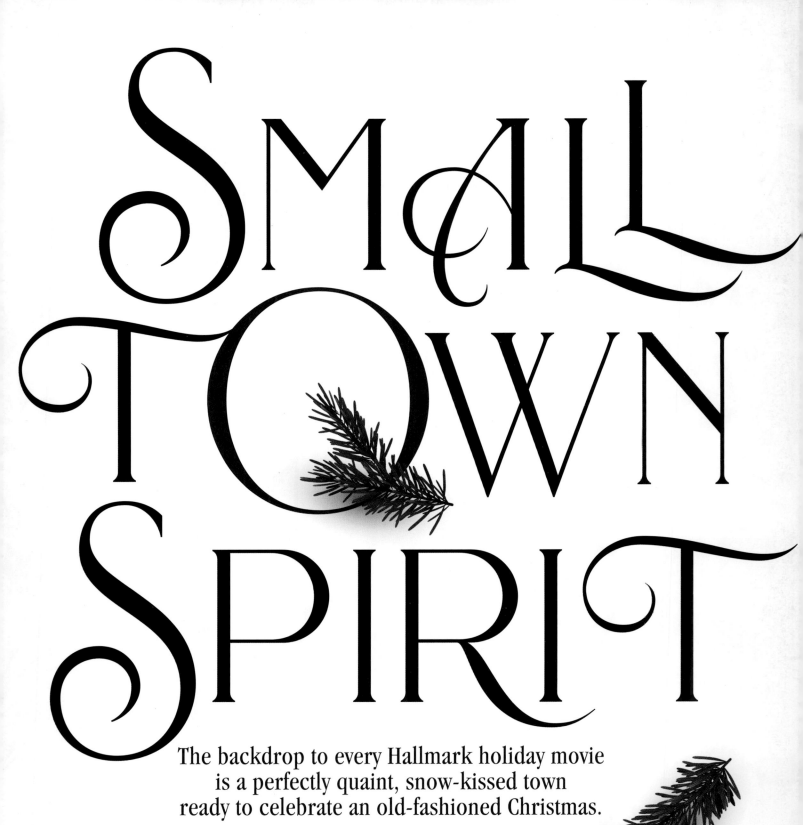

SMALL TOWN SPIRIT

The backdrop to every Hallmark holiday movie
is a perfectly quaint, snow-kissed town
ready to celebrate an old-fashioned Christmas.

THIS WAY TO CHRISTMAS

All signs point to merriment in Evergreen, the fictitious small town where the *Christmas in Evergreen* film series takes place.

TURNER'S TINKER SHOP

EVERGREEN EXPRESS

KRINGLE KITCHEN

POST OFFICE

DAISY'S COUNTRY STORE

CHURCH

BETWEEN THE TINSEL AND SPARKLE,

the piles of presents and the bottomless helpings of eggnog, Christmas is a time when more is more. (Especially when it comes to those trays upon trays of cookies—yum!) Yet, at the heart of every Hallmark Channel holiday movie is something decidedly small: a little town with a quaint main street and neighborly residents. From general stores and toy shops to ruby-red barns, these locations transform the movies into inviting walks down memory lane. They evoke the warm and fuzzy feelings that make Christmas special. "Every Hallmark movie wants—and needs!—that small cute town to give it the necessary sparkle," explains Jamie Lake, a production manager for numerous Hallmark films. Turn the page to dive into the many small towns where our favorite characters love, laugh, and connect.

ALL AGLOW

Evergreen's charming main street looks all the more magical when lit up with Christmas lights. Every Hallmark set shimmers with a minimum of 200 strands of lights, each featuring a meticulously counted 300 bulbs per strand.

THE MAIN ATTRACTION

Evergreen's idyllic main street is actually part of the Burnaby Village Museum in British Columbia. Before each filming, the set designers transform the landmark with hundreds of feet of garland and thousands of ornaments.

THOSE WALKS

down memory lane are all the more magical with the holiday element added to the mix. The Christmas preparations that pepper plots feel extra nostalgic when presented alongside a sweet small town.

Nowhere is that truer than in Evergreen, where a trio of movies—*Christmas in Evergreen, Christmas in Evergreen: Letters to Santa* and *Christmas in Evergreen: Tidings of Joy*— all take place. The fictitious Vermont town, said to be located "so far north that on clear days you might be able to see the North Pole," takes its inspiration from the work of iconic Hallmark artist Geoff Greenleaf. Indeed, with a post office, ice-cream parlor, and trolley all doused in powder-white snow, a picture-perfect Christmas-card scene is brought to life. (Fun fact: The movies are filmed at the Burnaby Village Museum in British Columbia.) As Evergreen resident and recurring character Allie (Ashley Williams) proclaims in the first film: "This is what Christmas is supposed to look like!"

SHOP LOCAL

In the second installment of the Evergreen series, *Christmas in Evergreen: Letters to Santa,* Lisa (Jill Wagner) returns to the town to discover the general store (left) has closed. She then leads a charge to reopen the beloved shop.

"EVERY HALLMARK

Christmas movie needs to feels like it could take place inside a snow globe."
—Chris McNally

Inviting as all Hallmark settings may be, the Evergreen franchise elevates that small-town sense of belonging, giving us a true familiarity from movie to movie. We also meet the neighbors, with recurring characters popping up across the Evergreen films: Mayor Green (Chris Cope), diner owners Carol and Joe (Barbara Niven and Malcolm Stewart), school principal Michelle (Holly Robinson Peete), inn owner Megan (Michelle Martin), choir director Hannah (Rukiya Bernard), farmer Henry (Daryl Shuttleworth), and a man named Nick (Keith Martin Gordey) who just happens to bear a striking resemblance to Santa Claus.

LET IT SNOW

Almost as integral as the characters themselves, snow brings a flurry of charm to Hallmark Christmas movies. The films have featured more than one million pounds of snow! Here, in a scene from *Christmas in Evergreen: Tidings of Joy*, Ezra (Chris Cope) finishes a snowman while Hannah (Rukiya Bernard) and Thomas (Colin Lawrence) get cozy and enjoy the winter fun.

SMALL-TOWN GATHERINGS
remind us of the comforts of the season—
togetherness, loyalty, and celebrating with loved ones.

The repeated presence of these friendly, utterly delightful townspeople lets us tag along as would-be members of a tight-knit community where helping, respecting, and connecting with those around you is all but a given—and not only during the most wonderful time of year.

As we slow down to watch the movies, we're transported to a time and place where a slower pace reigns. The holidays suddenly feel less like chaos and chores, and more like what they truly are: something to be cherished. Through small-town moments such as Christmas parades and tree lightings, we're reminded of the constants and comforts of the holidays—togetherness, loyalty, and celebrating alongside the people you love. In other words, the parts of Christmas that are truly evergreen.

COME TOGETHER

Small-town gatherings, like this tree lighting in *Our Christmas Love Song*, bring characters together and celebrate the spirit of community.

RINGLE KITCHEN

TEST YOUR CHRISTMAS IQ!
Can you ID the *Evergreen* films these scenes come from? Answers on page 218.

CHARACTER BUILDING

Because we revisit the town of Evergreen across the film series, the residents are as integral as the leading ladies and gentlemen. Even the scenery plays an important recurring role. From the park gazebo (the epicenter of the town's annual holiday festival) to farmer Miller's beaming red barn, Evergreen's landmarks are as familiar to us as those in our own hometowns. It makes watching the films feel as if we're strolling our local streets and catching up with dear old friends!

Letters to Santa

CHRIS KRINGLE KITCHEN

THE STRIDE STUDIOS

PICKUP LINE
Evergreen regular Allie (Ashley Williams) idles down the main street in her signature red pickup truck. The actress took lessons to learn to drive a stick shift for the role.

> **"**
>
> My favorite way to get
> into the holiday
> spirit is holiday baking,
> Elf on the Shelf,
> and family get-togethers.
>
> **"**

—**TAMERA MOWRY-HOUSLEY,**
STAR OF
A CHRISTMAS MIRACLE

HEART TO HEART

Tamera Mowry-Housley, shown here with Gabriel Jacob-Cross, in *A Christmas Miracle*.

THE WINTER GAMES

Residents of Oliver Wells, Virginia, gather for the annual snowman-building competition in *Christmas on Honeysuckle Lane*. Sparks fly between Emma (Alicia Witt) and Morgan (Colin Ferguson). Below: Emma is standing behind their snow creation, and Morgan (in a tan coat) is kneeling in front of it.

PERFECT HARMONY

In *A Christmas Miracle*, journalist Emma (Tamera Mowry-Housley) lands a cover story that proves life-changing for a lonely local street musician known as Santa Dean (Barry Bostwick, back to camera). Along the way, she and her colleague Marcus (Brooks Darnell) write their own unexpected love story.

CREATING THE PERFECT SET

Hallmark production designer Mark Boyko shares
his secrets to finding and fashioning Christmas-ready locations.

Q: How do you go about tracking down the small-town locations in which the movies are filmed?

A: You won't find many back lot sets on a Hallmark movie! We travel far and wide with boots-on-the-ground research to scout for each movie. Sometimes there are guiding story elements like "must have a general store." But it's typically a gut read on the charm and character of a place that guides our decision-making.

Q: Do you repeat some film locations? How do you differentiate them from movie to movie?

A: You'd be amazed by the tricks we have up our sleeves. Simply changing the color scheme, rearranging the furniture, or switching the camera angle can completely transform a space.

Q: Snow is a given. How do you make it happen?

A: We try to use actual snow whenever we can. Since we often film in the summer, sometimes fake is necessary. (We have an eco formula that would fool you as the real deal.) No matter the type, a snowball fight almost always breaks out on the set. I may have thrown a few myself!

Q: How long does it take to decorate those stunning on-screen trees?

A: Many hours! But it's a favorite task in the art department, so we don't mind. We do it as a group; it's our own little Christmas tradition.

ALL IN THE DETAILS Before filming begins on any Hallmark movie, imaginative set designers swoop in to transform the already picturesque locations into twirled-up holiday scenes. Decking the halls goes beyond the requisite Christmas tree to include decorating every inch of the sets: storefronts, streetlights, barns, cars, and sleighs. Thousands of feet of garland are hung. The saying "the more the merrier" has never been more fitting!

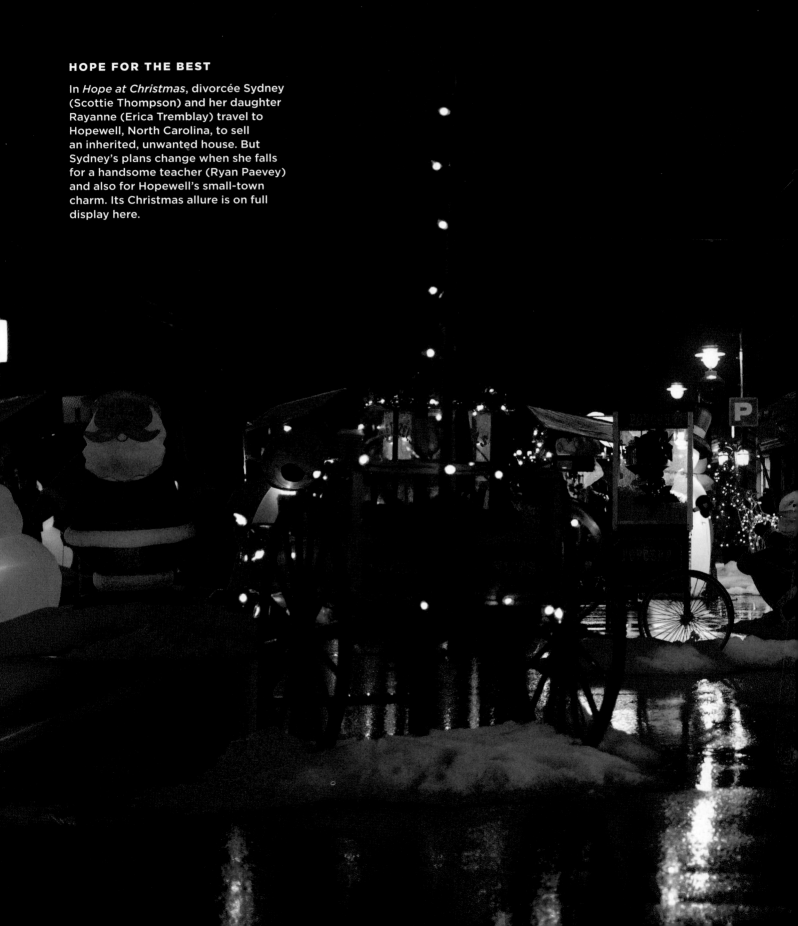

HOPE FOR THE BEST

In *Hope at Christmas*, divorcée Sydney (Scottie Thompson) and her daughter Rayanne (Erica Tremblay) travel to Hopewell, North Carolina, to sell an inherited, unwanted house. But Sydney's plans change when she falls for a handsome teacher (Ryan Paevey) and also for Hopewell's small-town charm. Its Christmas allure is on full display here.

MAKE A SECOND BATCH

In the season of giving, nothing evokes neighborly warmth more than a homemade treat, prepared and packaged with love.

FROM THE HEART

Jen Lilley and Lacey Chabert decorate Christmas cookies.

DANICA McKELLAR'S
QUINOA-BANANA BREAD

66 Gluten-free banana bread is my go-to. I started moving away from gluten
several years ago (despite my yearly chocolate Yule log, see page 182!), and I
found this recipe that uses quinoa flour and quinoa flakes instead of wheat flour.
It doubles well—and there is usually a desire for more! 99

ACTIVE 15 minutes / **TOTAL** 40 minutes / **MAKES** about 8 servings

INGREDIENTS

Butter or oil for greasing
the pan

½ cup quinoa flour

½ cup quinoa flakes (found in
the cereal or baking aisle)

2 tsp baking soda

1 tsp baking powder

½ tsp salt (or less)

2 very ripe, large bananas
(or 3 small ripe ones)

2 eggs

2 Tbsp honey or maple syrup

INSTRUCTIONS

1 Heat the oven to 400°F and grease a loaf pan with butter or oil.

2 In a large bowl, mix together the quinoa flour, quinoa flakes, baking
soda, baking powder, and salt. Set aside.

3 In a separate small bowl, mash the bananas. Add the eggs and honey,
and combine using a mixer or by hand. Add the wet ingredients to the
dry ingredients and mix again until well blended.

4 Pour the batter into the prepared loaf pan and bake until golden brown
on top and a toothpick or thin knife comes out clean, about 20 to
25 minutes. Yum!

Chocolate and Cranberry Fudge

66 In *Merry & Bright*, I played an expert candymaker, so I had to work to make it look like I knew my way around a kitchen and could pour melted chocolate into candy molds without making a mess! **99** —Jodie Sweetin

ACTIVE 35 minutes, plus infusing / **TOTAL** 35 minutes, plus infusing / **MAKES** about 2 pounds

INGREDIENTS

Butter or oil for greasing the pan

2 Tbsp orange liqueur

1 cup dried cranberries

3½ cups raw sugar

14 ounces condensed milk

1 stick salted butter

2 Tbsp cocoa powder, sifted

1 tsp pure vanilla extract

INSTRUCTIONS

1 Put the liqueur and cranberries in a small bowl; cover and leave to infuse overnight.

2 Grease a nonstick pan measuring about 7 inches square.

3 Put the sugar in a deep, heavy saucepan (at least 6 inches deep, as the mixture will bubble up considerably) with ¾ cup water, the condensed milk, butter, and cocoa powder. Heat slowly until the sugar has dissolved completely. Wash any sugar crystals down the side of the pan with a pastry brush dipped in water. Increase the heat and boil the syrup to the soft ball state (240°F on a candy thermometer). To test, drop a teaspoon of the mixture into a small bowl of cold water. Bring it together with your fingers and it should form a soft ball. Immediately take the pan off the heat and dip the base into cold water to stop the temperature of the syrup from rising further.

4 Let the syrup rest in the pan for 1 to 2 minutes, then use a wooden spoon to stir in the vanilla extract and cranberries. Continue stirring until the syrup starts to grain and stiffen. Before it thickens too much, pour it into the prepared pan.

5 While it is still warm, mark the fudge into squares. When cool, cut into pieces. Place in cone-shaped cellophane bags lined with waxed paper.

"I usually give out a tin of homemade candy using my grandmother's recipe. Our little elf even made a batch for himself this past Christmas."

—LACEY CHABERT

Chocolate & Cranberry Fudge

Chocolate & Cranberry Fudge

ALEXA PENAVEGA'S
CHRISTMAS CARAMEL CANDY

66 My favorite holiday gift? Hands down, homemade caramels. They are so fun to make, and who doesn't want a delicious treat that you took the time to make for them? I order candy wrappers online, and I wrap each caramel and place them in a mason jar for gifting! 99

ACTIVE 25 minutes / **TOTAL** 2 hours / **MAKES** about 4 dozen candies

INGREDIENTS

Butter or oil for greasing the pan

2 cups white sugar

1¾ cups corn syrup

1 cup whipping cream, divided

1 cup half-and-half, divided

1 cup butter

1 tsp vanilla

INSTRUCTIONS

1 Butter a 9-by-13-inch pan.

2 In a large pot over medium heat, combine the sugar, corn syrup, ½ cup whipping cream, ½ cup half-and-half, and butter. Bring to a boil.

3 Stir in the rest of the cream and half-and-half a little at a time. Do not let the mixture stop boiling.

4 When a candy thermometer reads 240°F, turn off the heat and add vanilla.

5 Pour the mixture into the pan. While it is still warm, mark the caramel into squares. When cool, cut into pieces. Wrap individual caramel pieces in candy wrappers or wax paper.

CRANBERRY SHORTBREAD

66 I love simple holiday cookies. Now that I have a 3-year-old daughter, we enjoy baking together. The whole kitchen is covered in sprinkles! **99**
—Lacey Chabert

ACTIVE 20 minutes / **TOTAL** 1 hour 30 minutes / **MAKES** 2 dozen cookies

INGREDIENTS

- ⅓ cup sugar
- ¼ tsp chopped fresh rosemary
- ⅓ cup frozen cranberries (about 1½ ounces)
- ¾ cup unsalted butter (1½ sticks), at room temp
- ½ tsp pure vanilla extract
- 1 tsp finely grated orange zest
- 1½ cups all-purpose flour
- ¼ tsp Kosher salt

INSTRUCTIONS

1 Line two baking sheets with parchment paper.

2 In a food processor, pulse the sugar and rosemary until very finely chopped. Transfer to the bowl of an electric mixer. Wipe out the food processor, add the frozen cranberries, and pulse to break up into pea-size pieces.

3 Add the butter to the rosemary sugar and beat on medium speed until very well combined. Beat in the vanilla and zest.

4 Reduce the mixer speed to low and gradually add the flour and salt, mixing until just incorporated. Add the chopped cranberries and mix to combine. The dough should look streaky with bits of cranberries.

5 On a piece of plastic wrap, form the dough into a rectangle measuring 7½ by 2¾ inches and 1 inch thick. Freeze or refrigerate until firm (about 45 minutes in the freezer or 2 hours in the fridge).

6 Heat the oven to 325°F. Slice the cookies ¼ inch thick and arrange on the prepared baking sheets, 2 inches apart. Bake, rotating the pans once, until the edges are light golden brown, 15 to 18 minutes. Let cool.

DEBBIE MATENOPOULOS'S
MOM'S ZUCCHINI BREAD

❝ My favorite bread to make is my mom's zucchini bread. For an
added treat, she would add dark chocolate chips. It is so delicious! **❞**

ACTIVE 15 minutes / **TOTAL** 1 hour 15 minutes / **MAKES** about 8 servings

INGREDIENTS

Oil for greasing the pan

3 eggs

2 cups granulated sugar

1 cup vegetable oil

2 cups grated, peeled raw zucchini

3 tsp pure vanilla extract

3 cups all-purpose flour

1 tsp salt

1 tsp baking soda

¼ tsp double-acting baking powder

3 tsp ground cinnamon

INSTRUCTIONS

1 Heat the oven to 350°F and grease two 9-by-5-inch loaf
pans with oil. Set aside.

2 In a large bowl, beat the eggs until light and foamy.
Add the sugar, oil, zucchini, and vanilla, and mix until
blended. Set aside.

3 In a separate bowl, combine the flour, salt, baking soda,
baking powder, and cinnamon; add the dry ingredients
to the egg-zucchini mixture and stir until well combined.

4 Pour the batter into the prepared pans. Bake until
golden brown on top and a toothpick or thin knife comes
out clean, about 1 hour. Remove the breads from the
oven and cool on a rack.

HEAD TO THE TREE FARM

It just doesn't feel like Christmas until there's a decked-out tree. The search for your perfect evergreen starts here.

You want a

FRESH TREE

Pros The natural scent will fill your home, and you are supporting farmers. You can feel good about getting a real tree, says Mike Bondi, a forestry and Christmas tree extension agent and forestry professor at Oregon State University. Grown primarily on family farms that employ local workers, the trees are a renewable crop—more are planted than harvested. Plus, they can be chipped or mulched and composted. (To find a recycling program, visit *earth911.com* and type in "Christmas trees" and your zip code.) You can also donate them to a group that uses trees to shore up beach dunes; go to *christmastree.org/all-about-trees/how-to-recycle* for info.

Cons You can keep a cut tree inside for only three to six weeks, and you must be diligent about watering it. If it gets dry and is exposed to frayed lights, it could be a fire hazard. (To prevent this, inspect lights annually.) And because trees drop needles, you'll have to vacuum a lot.

IDENTIFICATION KEY

EVERGREENS

Separate the firs from the pines with this guide to common live conifers.

BALSAM FIR The most fragrant of all, these dry out easily, so be sure to watch your watering.

BLUE SPRUCE Its blue hue offers a tonal twist on the usual color scheme.

DOUGLAS FIR These all-stars have a full shape that fills larger spaces easily.

FRASER FIR Sturdy branches, minimal shedding, and a strong scent make them a trifecta.

SCOTCH PINE Minimal shedding and high water retention make these a low-maintenance choice.

SILVER TIP Their open growth pattern offers more space to show off decorations.

VIRGINIA PINE Popular in the South, their branches are dense yet easily trimmable.

TIP:
If your tree
seems to stop drawing
water during the holidays,
help it drink more easily
by making a few slits in
the bark below the water
line with a keyhole
saw or a serrated
knife.

HOW TO FIND ONE

Want a fresh tree but not sure where to shop? You can visit *christmastree.org* and type in your zip code to find a retail lot or farm in your area.

WHAT TO DO AT THE TREE FARM

Measure it. Choose a tree that's six inches to one foot shorter than your ceiling, leaving room for a topper and a tree stand, recommends John Perry, who has been growing Christmas trees for decades at Yuletide Tree Farm in New Egypt, New Jersey. "Remember," Perry says, "the farm has a limitless ceiling and trees look shorter in the field than they do in a house." Also, don't forget to measure the tree's diameter to make sure it will fit in your space.

Tie it. Ask the tree farm staff to shake the tree free of loose needles and wrap it in netting. If the farm doesn't have netting, tie a sturdy rope to the trunk of the tree and then wrap it all around the branches (pointed up) to the top to make it easier to handle.

Hoist it. After spreading a blanket on your car's roof to protect the paint, lift the tree onto the roof with its base at the front of the car to minimize wind damage. Wrap the blanket around the tree.

Secure it. If your car has a roof rack, wrap twine around it and the blanketed tree. If not, use Perry's method: Open your car doors and pass twine from the driver's-side front seat diagonally over the tree and through the passenger's-side back door. Then, bring the twine to the driver's-side back door, up diagonally over the tree and through the passenger's-side front door, forming an X over the tree. Then tie the ends.

WHAT TO DO WHEN YOU GET YOUR TREE HOME

Cut it. Remove ½ to ¾ inch from the bottom of the tree before putting it in the stand. This is to expose fresh, open cells for water absorption, Bondi says. (You can skip this step if your tree was first cut within the past two hours.)

Water it. Secure the tree in a stand with a one-gallon reservoir and fill it to the top with fresh water. During the first week, the tree can absorb half a gallon or more of water each day, so remember to refill it often. And you can skip additives like sugar, beer, or bleach. Despite what you may have heard or read online, nothing works better than fresh water, Bondi says.

You want a LIVING TREE

Pro Wrapped in soil and burlap, a tree that has its roots still intact can be planted outside after Christmas is over. That makes it an environmentally friendly choice.

Cons You can keep a living tree indoors for only one or two weeks. Heated air tricks the tree into thinking it's spring, so it sprouts new shoots and has a lower chance of surviving outside. Plus, if you live in a cold climate, the hole you'll plant it in has to be dug before the ground freezes.

WHERE TO FIND ONE

Your local garden center is likely your best bet for finding a living tree. Or you might consider renting a tree. The Living Christmas Company (*livingchristmas.com*), for example, delivers potted pines and spruces to Californians, then picks them up after the Christmas season is over and repots the trees so that they can be put to use again next holiday season.

HOW TO CHOOSE THE BEST TREE

Before settling on a tree, be sure to check it out for freshness. "Grab a branch," recommends Rick Dungey, executive director of the National Christmas Tree Association. "If it bends, it's fresh. If it snaps, move on, because it's brittle and dried out."

"

We have a family tradition of the great Christmas tree hunt! We roam our hillsides on the Saturday after Thanksgiving to find the perfect tree, which always ends up being far too big for the car and the house, but nonetheless we end up making the same mistake year after year!

—**KEN WINGARD,** *HOME & FAMILY* LIFESTYLE AND HOME FURNISHINGS MASTER EXPERT

"

You want a FAKE TREE

Pros No watering or vacuuming needles; some even include lights. And if you use it for five to 10 years, your investment pays off. (Candace Cameron Bure says she's a recent convert to fake trees: "I don't think I'll ever go back!")
Cons It has to be disassembled and stored in a cool, dry area. And it can never be recycled, so one day it will end up in a landfill.

HOW TO PICK ONE

Look closely at the tree's branches, which are made of either PVC or more expensive PE plastic. Good-quality PVC will have needles that blend in with the trunk or branches.

(If you are buying online, be sure to zoom in on the picture.) The more branch tips or "needles" the faux tree has, the more authentic it will look. One good guideline for finding a believable-looking tree is looking for a seven-foot tree with 1,200 branch tips. You may also want to opt for a metal stand, which is sturdier than plastic.

WHERE TO FIND ONE

Try *treetopia.com* if you're after an affordable and funky tree, such as a pink, red, or blue one. Prefer a more classic tree? You'll find a range at *balsamhill.com*.

CHAPTER 2

CELEBRATE WITH THE ONES YOU LOVE

WONDER WOMEN

At the heart of every Hallmark holiday
movie is a leading lady who is strong, principled,
and not above a good snowball fight.

ALL IN THE FAMILY

Patti LaBelle and Holly Robinson Peete went from co-stars to lifelong friends after appearing together in *A Family Christmas Gift.* The two now love to swap recipes. (Robinson Peete swears by LaBelle's macaroni and cheese; see page 208 for the recipe!)

Ladies First

This old-fashioned adage applies perfectly to Hallmark Christmas movies, where smart, relatable heroines with 1,000-watt smiles serve as our entry point into the holiday magic. As actor Teddy Sears explains of his *Christmas in Evergreen* co-star Ashley Williams, and of Hallmark leading ladies in general: "Her face becomes Christmas. It's a perfect, smiley, bright-eyed look of wonder that can make a whole movie shine." Whether the main character is a career-focused professional, such as Candace Cameron Bure's Lauren in *Christmas Under Wraps*, or a spunky creative, like Tia Mowry-Hardrict as Taylor the architect in *A Gingerbread Romance*, she is our on-screen alter ego. These actresses draw us in to a world we're all longing to be a part of, where community, friendship, and hope thrive amongst the glow of twinkling Christmas. Better still, these female leads are no shrinking poinsettias. "One of the most unique aspects about working with the Hallmark Channel is the emphasis placed on developing strong female protagonists. These characters are empowered," explains longtime network screenwriter Tracy Andreen. Through their Christmastime exploits—and spirited transformations—we're able to connect with intelligent, value-driven women who, in turn, open our hearts to the real meaning of the holiday season.

CHEER LEADER

Candace Cameron Bure's 2014 film *Christmas Under Wraps* set a viewing record with 8 million fans tuning in for the premiere.

ALONG THE WAY

the movies also introduce us to loving, salt-of-the-earth family and neighbors—and, let's not forget, a dreamy leading man. They're all people anyone would love to spend the holidays with.

Speaking of spending time together, the Hallmark heroines feel like family. With a rotating roster of stars, including Candace Cameron Bure, Lacey Chabert, Patti LaBelle, Jen Lilley, Danica McKellar, Tamera Mowry-Housley, Holly Robinson Peete, Jodie Sweetin, Jill Wagner, Ashley Williams, and Alicia Witt, these festive films make you feel as if you're catching up with an old friend. "I always include a tree-decorating scene in every script," says Andreen. "It creates a moment where viewers can prep for the season and get into the holiday spirit right alongside their favorite actresses!"

ALL THE TRIMMINGS

Lisa (Jill Wagner) helps Evergreen newcomer Katie (Maggie Lawson) decorate a town tree in *Christmas in Evergreen: Tidings of Joy.*

$\mathcal{A}$s in Real Life,

the leading ladies are able to laugh about their blunders and embarrassing moments. Maybe that's why they remind us of our cherished friends and ourselves.

One reason that these holiday movies make us feel so nostalgic is the fact that many of the stars appeared in beloved shows from our younger days—McKellar was Winnie on *The Wonder Years*, and Cameron Bure and Sweetin played D.J. and Stephanie Tanner on *Full House*, to name just a few examples.

Their more recent star turns in Hallmark holiday movies aren't just for *our* viewing pleasure. The actresses also delight in portraying the cozy, homey holiday scenes we all love so well. "Hallmark has really become like family," explains Chabert, whose hits include *A Royal Christmas* and *A Christmas Melody*. "Each film is like a reunion. I am blessed to be a part of something that brings some joy to people and adds a little bit of goodness back into the world."

HOLLY DOLLY CHRISTMAS

Danica McKellar pinched herself while performing alongside the legendary Dolly Parton in *Christmas at Dollywood*. McKellar says she had to relearn the Electric Slide for the movie. "It finally came back from my teen years!" she says.

CREATURE COMFORTS

Does Candace Cameron Bure have a favorite Hallmark movie? She'll never tell! But the actress does admit to having a soft spot for those that include four-legged co-stars. Here, she cuddles with a fluffy friend in *Christmas Town*.

A HALLMARK HEROINE

finds the fun in holiday rituals, trades witty
banter with confidence, and looks nothing short of fierce
whether she's wearing a parka or a party dress.

THE SHOW MUST GO ON

Actress Christina Milian made her
Hallmark debut playing career-
focused Noelle in *Memories
of Christmas*. Here, she dons
her soirée best and comes to
the rescue of her hometown's
beloved Christmas gala.

Being surrounded by Christmas
spirit all year long while filming is a recipe
for friendship and community. There's a deep
bond between many of the actresses, who
have become close friends over the years.
"We promote and rally around one another.
What's better than supporting another woman?
I'm honored to be a part of this group," says
Chabert.

Witt adds, "It's fun to come out with a movie
where you spend your days in cheery winter
clothes, with Christmas lights everywhere and
snow on the ground and gingerbread cookies
and vegan eggnog at the ready. How can there
be any heaviness to your psyche when you're
surrounded by all that?"

TEST YOUR CHRISTMAS IQ!
Which photos are from films with Christmas in the title? For answers, see page 218.

CASTING A LEADING LADY

Penny Perry, Hallmark's senior vice president of casting, gives the inside scoop on finding just the right actress for each role.

Q: What are the essential qualities every Hallmark actress should possess, no matter the plotline?

A: The leads in our films are almost always strong female characters, so the actresses have to have lots of attributes and experiences they can pull from. We look for actresses who are warm, charming, likable, captivating, and most important, relatable.

Q: Hallmark movies are known for repeat performances from certain actresses. How do you decide which project is right for which star?

A: We closely read scripts in development to determine what storylines best match up with a particular actress's style and charisma. (They are all unique, after all!) Once cast, we sometimes layer elements of her personality into the script.

Q: The female leads are especially beloved by fans. Why do you think that is the case?

A: Every actress we cast has to be able to emotionally connect with our audiences. The actresses also have to be funny and able to tackle humorous banter. Who doesn't like a heroine who can make you laugh? Lastly, there has to be chemistry between the leads so the romance pops on screen.

SEEING RED No matter the story, red is the signature color of actresses in Hallmark Christmas movies—from scarves to gowns, and even the occasional jumpsuit! In many of the films, crimson coats and puffy jackets brighten up the most enchanting winter scenes. It's the color of good cheer, after all, and it makes our heroines easy to spot as the stars of every festive scene.

Jodie
Sweetin

Lacey
Chabert

Tatyana
Ali

Holly
Robinson
Peete

Candace
Cameron
Bure

Becca
Tobin

GOLDEN GIRL
Tony Award winner Kristin Chenoweth hits just the right note as Katherine, a Broadway star turned school choir director in Hallmark Hall of Fame's *A Christmas Love Story*. Chenoweth was drawn to the role because she relates to the character's passion for improving lives through music.

FOR HE'S A JOLLY GOOD FELLOW

Accompanying every heroine is an equally secure leading man. Resilient, honorable, and big-hearted, the guys offer steadfast comfort and warmth. From the sweet first encounter to the end-of-the-movie kiss, the love interest supports the female character on her arc of discovery and growth. (Naturally, they both supply plenty of flirty exchanges and on-screen chemistry along the way!)

With good looks, good manners, and good intentions, these fellows steal our own hearts movie after movie. Read on for a few of our favorite gentlemen in their standout Hallmark holiday roles.

MAN UP

Fan favorite Andrew Walker's
seasonal traditions include
family caroling and plenty of
sweets. Walker's Christmas film
hits include *Merry & Bright* and
Christmas on My Mind.

MERRY MEN

These six magnetic actors bring an extra shot of joy to the movies in which they co-star.

1. DENNIS HAYSBERT
CHRISTMAS EVERLASTING

Uncle Barney (Dennis Haysbert) is a rock for his bereaved niece Lucy (Tatyana Ali). Plus, sparks fly between him and Mrs. Swinson (Patti LaBelle, shown here).

2. DREW SEELEY
A CHRISTMAS FOR THE BOOKS

TV producer Ted (Drew Seeley) goes from host Joanna's (Chelsea Kane) pretend boyfriend to the real deal.

3. JESSE METCALFE
CHRISTMAS UNDER THE STARS

Investment banker turned Christmas-tree-lot employee Nick (Jesse Metcalfe) learns a lesson in love from astronomy teacher Julie (Autumn Reeser).

4. CHAD MICHAEL MURRAY
ROAD TO CHRISTMAS

Los Angeles producer Maggie (Jessy Schram) flips for Danny (Chad Michael Murray) while on assignment in Vermont.

5. MARK DEKLIN
CHRISTMAS IN EVERGREEN: LETTERS TO SANTA

Contractor Kevin (Mark Deklin) works with retail designer Lisa (Jill Wagner) to save Evergreen's general store.

6. MARK TAYLOR
MEMORIES OF CHRISTMAS

Noelle (Christina Milian) returns home and finds love with Christmas-light installer David (Mark Taylor).

SEASONS EATINGS

Serving treasured family recipes along
with new favorites makes festive gatherings all the
more memorable.

DYNAMIC DUO

Debbie Matenopoulos and Cameron Mathison cook up a seasonal spread on *Home & Family*.

DANICA MCKELLAR'S
Dry-Brined Turkey

66 This turkey is *so* tender and flavorful. I tried it for the first time last year, and I'll never do a turkey any other way. My mom has an herb garden, so I used sage, rosemary, and thyme fresh from the backyard. **99**

ACTIVE 15 minutes / **TOTAL** 2 to 3 days / **MAKES** 1 serving per pound of turkey

INGREDIENTS

- 1 whole turkey
- 2 Tbsp Kosher salt
- 2 Tbsp seasonings, such as chopped herbs

INSTRUCTIONS

1 Remove the turkey from the plastic and pat it very dry. No need to rinse it.

2 Mix together the salt and your chosen seasonings. Place the turkey on a rimmed baking sheet, then rub the salt mixture all over. Place the turkey and baking sheet together in a plastic bag (use two if necessary) and refrigerate.

3 Let the brine sit on the bird at least overnight or up to two days for a medium bird (12 to 14 pounds) and up to three days for a larger turkey before roasting as usual following your favorite recipe.

ALEXA AND CARLOS PENAVEGA'S
Sancocho Stew

" We are Colombian and Dominican, so our holiday meals have to have our Hispanic flair. We make 'sancocho'—a stew with *all* sorts of goodies! **"**

ACTIVE 15 minutes / **TOTAL** 55 minutes / **MAKES** about 10 to 12 servings

INGREDIENTS

- 1 pound boneless chicken thighs, cut into chunks
- 1 pound boneless pork shoulder, trimmed and cut into chunks
- 1 pound boneless short ribs
- 1 Tbsp garlic powder
- 1 Tbsp onion powder
- 1 Tbsp ground annatto (optional)
- 1 tsp ground cumin
- 2 tsp Kosher salt
- 2 tsp freshly ground pepper
- 2 Tbsp finely chopped garlic (or more if desired!)
- 1 large onion, chopped
- 1 celery stalk, chopped
- 2 small bunches cilantro, chopped
- 3 russet potatoes, peeled and cut into chunks
- 3 yuccas (cassava root), peeled and cut into chunks
- 2 Tbsp rice vinegar
- 2 Tbsp lemon juice
  Cooked rice, for serving
  Cooked corn, for serving (optional)
  Chopped cilantro, for serving
- 4 scallions, chopped, for serving

INSTRUCTIONS

1 In a large pot or Dutch oven, toss the meat with the garlic and onion powders, ground annatto, if using, cumin, salt, and pepper. Toss with the garlic, onion, celery, and cilantro. Add enough water to cover all the ingredients (about 2 quarts) and bring to a boil.

2 Add the potato, yucca, and vinegar; return to a boil, stirring every few minutes. Reduce the heat and simmer until the meat is very tender, 45 to 60 minutes, adding more water as necessary.

3 Stir in lemon juice. Serve over rice with corn, if desired. Sprinkle with cilantro and scallions.

DEBBIE MATENOPOULOS'S
Brussels Sprouts With Chestnuts

66 I start serving Brussels sprouts with chestnuts around Thanksgiving and make them through the New Year. They're outrageously delicious and a favorite at every gathering. 99

ACTIVE 25 minutes / **TOTAL** 55 minutes / **MAKES** 12 servings

INGREDIENTS

- 1 pound Brussels sprouts—washed, trimmed, outer leaves removed, quartered
- 2 Tbsp olive oil or grapeseed oil
  Kosher salt and freshly ground black pepper, to taste
- 1 medium shallot, thinly sliced
- ⅓ cup chopped steamed chestnuts
- ¼ cup freshly grated Parmesan cheese

INGREDIENTS FOR TRUFFLE BUTTER

- 1 stick butter, softened
  Zest and juice of ½ lemon
- ¼ tsp truffle salt

INSTRUCTIONS

1 Heat oven to 450°F. In a large bowl, toss the Brussels sprouts with oil and season with salt, and pepper.

2 Place a large cast-iron skillet over high heat. When hot, place the Brussels sprouts cut-side down in a single layer. Cook without stirring until caramelized, about 4 minutes. Add the shallots and chestnuts, and sauté a couple minutes more.

3 Place the skillet in the oven on the top rack and roast until crispy, 10 to 20 minutes, stirring halfway through cooking.

4 While the Brussels sprouts roast, make the truffle butter. In a small food processor, combine the butter, lemon zest and juice, and truffle salt, and process until well blended.

5 Remove the skillet from the oven. When still hot, top the cooked Brussels sprouts with the truffle butter and Parmesan.

AL ROKER'S
Family Sweet Potatoes

❝ The one recipe I love to make is my mother's sweet potato poon. It is a crustless sweet potato pie with a big marshmallow top. It always reminds me of her and Christmas. ❞

ACTIVE 25 minutes / **TOTAL** 55 minutes / **MAKES** about 12 servings

INGREDIENTS

Butter for greasing the pan

6 large sweet potatoes, about 4 pounds total, peeled and cut into 2-inch cubes

8 Tbsp (1 stick) unsalted butter, cut into pieces

1 cup all-purpose flour

1 cup firmly packed dark brown sugar

¼ cup baking powder

1 tsp ground cinnamon

1 tsp freshly ground nutmeg

1 tsp ground allspice

1 tsp Kosher salt

1 cup crushed pineapple, drained

1 12-ounce bag marshmallows

INSTRUCTIONS

1 Heat the oven to 350°F. Butter a 9-by-12-inch glass baking dish.

2 Bring a large pot of water to a boil over high heat. Add the sweet potatoes and cook until soft, about 12 minutes. Drain the potatoes and transfer to a large bowl. Add the butter and mash the potatoes with the butter. Stir in the flour, brown sugar, baking powder, cinnamon, nutmeg, allspice, and salt until well blended. Fold in the crushed pineapple and transfer to the prepared baking dish.

3 Bake until the sweet potatoes are brown on top, about 30 minutes. Remove from the oven and place the marshmallows in a single layer on top.

4 Heat the broiler and place the dish underneath the broiler to toast the marshmallows. Watch carefully as they will toast very fast!

KEN WINGARD'S
Grandma Etta's
Parker House Rolls

❝ This is my go-to dish to take to a holiday gathering. I started moving away from gluten a few years ago, but I make an exception for these. **❞**

ACTIVE 35 minutes / **TOTAL** 1 hour 15 minutes / **MAKES** 16 rolls

INGREDIENTS

- 1 cup boiling water
- ½ cup shortening
- ¼ cup plus 1 tsp sugar
- 1 tsp salt
- 1 package dry yeast
- ½ cup warm water (110°F)
- 1 egg
- 4 cups flour, divided
- ½ cup butter, melted
  Melted butter, sea salt flakes, and chopped herbs, for serving

INSTRUCTIONS

1 In a large bowl, combine the boiling water, shortening, ¼ cup sugar, and salt, and mix to combine. Set aside and let cool.

2 In a separate large bowl, dissolve the yeast and remaining sugar in the warm water. Add the egg and 2 cups of the flour and mix well.

3 Add the shortening mixture and the remaining flour to the dough; mix well. Cover and refrigerate overnight or until doubled in size.

4 Knead dough on a floured board and roll it out to ¼ inch thick. Cut into circles with a biscuit cutter or glass. Brush each roll with melted butter, then fold in half. Place rolls side by side in a pan. Cover and let rise in a warm place until doubled again.

5 When ready to bake, heat the oven to 400°F. Bake the rolls for 10 minutes.

6 Remove the rolls from the oven and brush with melted butter. Sprinke with sea salt and chopped herbs. Immediately hide so there will be some left for dinner.

SET TO SHINE

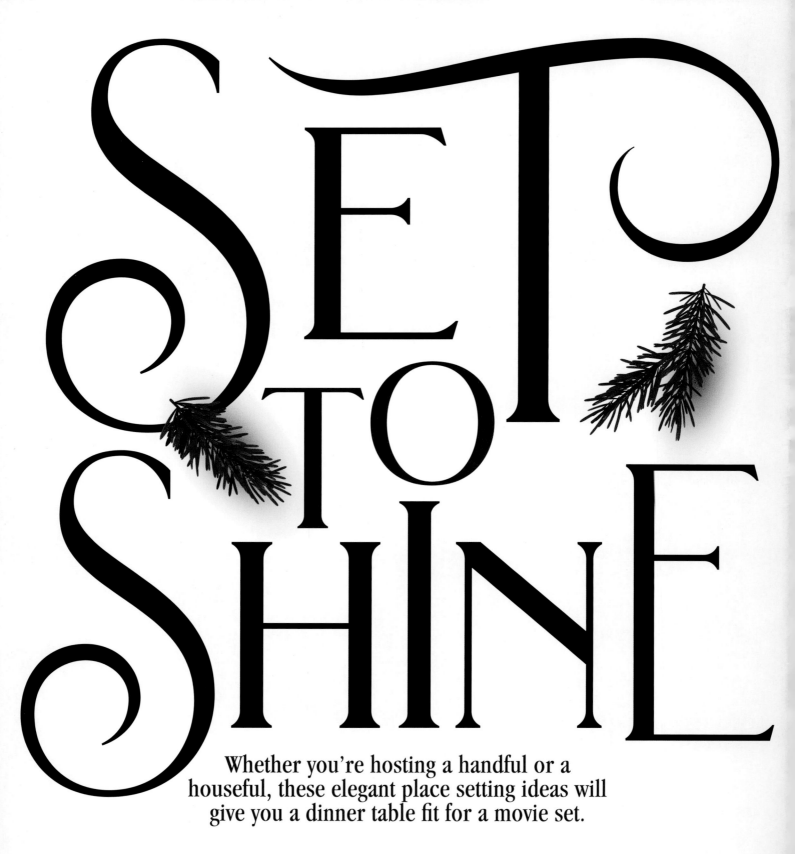

Whether you're hosting a handful or a
houseful, these elegant place setting ideas will
give you a dinner table fit for a movie set.

MAGICAL WORLD

A mix of finishes—copper, mercury glass, crystal, and more—bring a shimmering finish to this holiday tablescape.

Create

A HOMEY,
UTTERLY COZY
TABLESCAPE

1. START WITH SIMPLE GREENERY

Look no further than your backyard for your table runner. Wood slices add a rough-hewn touch and can also log time as chargers.

2. ADD A POP OF PLAID

A classic tartan tablecloth dresses up a space in a polished (but not pretentious) way.

3. TRY SOMETHING NEW

Splurge on one or two special touches for the table, whether it's double old-fashioned glasses or hand-thrown ceramic dinner plates.

4. INCORPORATE SOMETHING OLD

For whimsical place settings, slide handwritten name cards into the slots of vintage sleigh bells and give new meaning to "be there with bells on." (Guests can take them home as favors.)

5. CAST A ROSY GLOW

Frosted-bulb string lights woven into the greenery add instant ambience, while candles in oversize mason jars cozy up the tablescape. Rose-gold flatware, a striking and more modern alternative to silver, warms things up even more.

Create
A Soulful Display

1. KEEP IT SWEET

Place red striped runners horizontally over a white tablecloth. Tie each folded napkin with red ribbon and tuck in one sprig of fir or pine.

2. GO EVERGREEN

Take your cue from *Christmas in Evergreen*: Set out a dessert station featuring a wintry white cake decorated with Christmas trees.

3. BE PRESENT

For a fun treat, set your holiday table and then top each person's plate with one small gift to open before the first course.

Create

EASY KRAFT PAPER PLACE SETTINGS

Transform your holiday dining table with a roll of kraft paper and minimal DIY skills. Bonus: No cranberry-stained table linens!

1. A CHIC BASKET-WEAVE DESIGN

For the center of the runner, cut an 18-inch-wide by 24-inch-long piece of kraft paper. Draw 1-inch lines along the width of the paper, leaving a 1-inch border on the shorter ends and a ½-inch border on the longer sides. Use a utility knife and ruler to cut along the lines. Thread 30 strips of paper (½ inch by 23 inches) through the slits in a basket-weave pattern. Secure the ends with tape and cut off the excess, then position the woven mat atop the center of a plain paper runner. Along with the woven mat, rose-gold flatware and earthy, clay-rimmed dinner plates use textures and finishes to elevated effect.

2. A SIMPLE, MODERN LOOK

Use a pencil to lightly draw three sides of a 16-inch square, leaving the top side open. Write each guest's name in the center of that space; extend the lines on both sides of the name to complete the square. Trace the pencil with a white paint marker and let dry. This tablescape complements marble and metallic linens.

3. WOODSY, RUSTIC CHARM

Layer a birch bark sheet (sold in craft supply stores) atop a kraft paper runner with a whip-stitched edge (made with a hole punch and colored twine). Pair with gingham and wood accents and outdoorsy place card holders.

CHAPTER 3

FIND YOUR CHRISTMAS SPIRIT

HERE COMES SANTA

No matter your age, no one inspires holiday
excitement quite like jolly old St. Nick.

SEASON'S GREETINGS

In *Christmas Wonderland*, a storefront Santa Claus is there to help Heidi (Emily Osment) celebrate an eagerly awaited career win.

Catching a glimpse of a certain Man in red

soaring through a winter evening sky may be a long shot.
But sit down to watch a Hallmark Christmas movie and the odds
suddenly turn in your favor. To date, Santa Claus has
appeared in nearly 100 of the films! That's no accident. His presence
instantly infuses a storyline with love, whimsy,
and, best of all, a bit of magic. "Santa has the ability to remind us of
our childhood and of simpler times. There is a wonderment
that he can have on our souls, no matter how old we grow,"
explains Hallmark director Jonathan Wright.

MAKE A WISH

In many favorite films, Santa Claus helps holiday dreams come true—from pined-for love to happy family news.

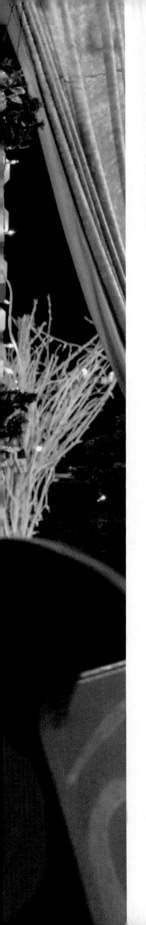

It's No Surprise

that regardless of how handsome the leading man may be, Santa Claus is the person who can make our heart skip a beat. While he is best known for delivering material things, the true gift he imparts is a lesson in the joy of giving, not getting. Whether he's teaching incorrigible children the importance of giving back (*Cancel Christmas*) or playing matchmaker (*A Boyfriend for Christmas*), Santa celebrates selflessness and love in a way no other character can.

His cheery, generous spirit simply can't be matched. "Santa Claus defines 'good' and, more than that, warms your heart with his jovial laugh and twinkling eyes. He can make even the humbugs believe," says Hallmark casting director Jackie Lind, who has cast her share of Kris Kringles. "A real beard is a must," she adds.

CHILD'S PLAY

In *A Bramble House Christmas*, Scout (Liam Hughes) sees his mother receive a windfall inheritance and welcome a wonderful new man into her life. A visit with Santa adds to the unforgettable Christmas season.

DEAR SANTA

In *Matchmaker Santa*, the titular (and very jolly!) character helps Melanie (Lacey Chabert, second from right) find her ideal love match just in time for Christmas. Cast members also shown, from left: Florence Henderson, Lin Shaye, John Ratzenberger, and Adam Mayfield.

'TIS THE SEASON
To be jolly. Ho, ho, ho!

Santa's merry ways can be contagious. Just ask Hallmark Channel host Debbie Matenopoulos, who once got so deeply into the Santa spirit that she set a record for the person who could dress the fastest in a Santa costume—hat, beard, gloves, boots, the whole getup. "I am now officially a record holder in *The Guinness Book of World Records*. Could there be anything more fun?" she says.

From his festive red suit to his decidedly selfless spirit, Santa's presence in Hallmark Christmas films celebrates the things that matter most: kindness, connection, and counting our many blessings.

MR. MAGIC

You can count on Santa to draw a crowd. Here, the jolly gift giver captivates Evergreen residents Thomas (Colin Lawrence), David (Marlon Kazadi), Hannah (Rukiya Bernard), and Michelle (Holly Robinson Peete) in a scene from *Christmas in Evergreen: Letters to Santa*.

SANTA SIGHTINGS

Sometimes the man in red is the main attraction. Sometimes he is simply a festive extra adding to the holiday atmosphere. Regardless of where he appears—or who is dressing up as him—he's sure to make us smile. Here, a few of the places Santa has popped up over the years: (top row, left to right) *A Bramble House Christmas*, *Mingle All the Way*, *Meet the Peetes*, *Marry Me at Christmas*; (middle row, left to right) *A Family for Christmas*, *Christmas Bells Are Ringing*, media appearance with Happy the Dog; (bottom row, left to right) *Hallmark Home & Family* Holiday Special, *Miss Christmas*, *The Mistletoe Inn*, *The Mistletoe Secret*.

LEAVE A TREAT FOR ST. NICK

Homemade cookies to set out for Santa—or to enjoy yourself!

COOKIE COUNTDOWN

It doesn't feel like December to Candace Cameron Bure without treats in the oven. Find her recipe for Chewy Ginger Cookies on page 122.

DEBBIE MATENOPOULOS'S CRANBERRY OATMEAL COOKIES

" My favorite cookie recipe for Santa is a relatively new addition given to me last year by my friend Bridgette. I made them over the holidays and they were a huge hit. **"**

ACTIVE 15 minutes / **TOTAL** 30 minutes / **MAKES** about 3 dozen cookies

INGREDIENTS

- ¾ cup unbleached all-purpose flour
- ½ cup firmly packed light brown sugar
- ¼ cup granulated sugar
- ½ tsp baking soda
- ¼ tsp salt
- ¼ tsp ground cinnamon
- 1 stick unsalted butter, melted
- 1 large egg, lightly beaten
- ½ tsp pure vanilla extract
- 1½ cups old-fashioned rolled oats
- ½ cup dried cranberries
- ¾ cup white chocolate chips

INSTRUCTIONS

1 Heat oven to 350°F. Line a baking sheet with parchment paper. Set aside.

2 In a large mixing bowl, whisk together the flour, brown sugar, sugar, baking soda, salt, and cinnamon.

3 Add the butter, egg, and vanilla to the flour mixture, mixing until combined. Fold in the oats, cranberries, and white chocolate chips.

4 Drop tablespoons of dough 3 inches apart onto the prepared cookie sheet. Bake until the edges are golden, about 11 to 13 minutes.

5 Transfer to a wire rack to cool.

SPRITZ COOKIES

❝ We leave Santa classic Christmas cookies with frosting. They're simple but always homemade, because I don't like the slice-and-bake kind. ❞ —Al Roker

ACTIVE 30 minutes / **TOTAL** 55 minutes, plus cooling and setting / **MAKES** about 5½ dozen cookies

INGREDIENTS

2¼ cups all-purpose flour

½ tsp baking powder

½ tsp salt

1 cup butter or margarine (2 sticks), softened

½ cup sugar

1 large egg

1 tsp vanilla extract

1 tsp almond extract

Candy décors (optional)

Royal icing (optional)

INSTRUCTIONS

1 Heat the oven to 350°F. Place two cookie sheets in the freezer.

2 On waxed paper, toss together the flour, baking powder, and salt.

3 In a large bowl, with a mixer on medium speed, beat the butter and sugar until pale and creamy. Beat in the egg, then both extracts. With the mixer on low, gradually add the flour mixture. Beat just until blended.

4 Spoon a third of the dough into a cookie press or large decorating bag fitted with a large star tip. Onto the chilled cookie sheets, press or pipe the dough into desired shapes, spacing 2 inches apart. Sprinkle with candy décors before baking, if using.

5 Bake the cookies until lightly browned around the edges, 10 to 12 minutes, rotating the cookie sheets between upper and lower oven racks halfway through. Place the cookie sheets on a wire rack to cool for 2 minutes. Transfer the cookies to the rack to cool completely. Rechill the cookie sheets and then repeat with the remaining dough.

6 Decorate the cookies as desired with royal icing and candies, if using. Set aside to allow the icing to dry.

7 Store the cookies in an airtight container for up to a week, or freeze up to a month.

CANDACE CAMERON BURE'S
CHEWY GINGER COOKIES

66 I *love* gingerbread everything! It's something I look forward to making come November! I got this chewy ginger cookie recipe from a sweet woman in Canada who baked them for the cast and crew while we were filming a Hallmark movie. They are so yummy, and I like that they have a chewy texture as opposed to the traditional hard gingerbread snap. **99**

ACTIVE 20 minutes / **TOTAL** 35 minutes / **MAKES** about 4 dozen cookies

INGREDIENTS

1½ cups oil (I use grapeseed oil)

2 cups sugar

2 eggs

¾ cup molasses

4 cups flour (I add an extra 4 Tbsp)

4 tsp baking soda

1 Tbsp ground ginger

2 tsp cinnamon

1 tsp ground cloves

1 tsp salt

Raw or white sugar for rolling cookies

INSTRUCTIONS

1 In a large bowl, combine oil, sugar, eggs, and molasses.

2 Add the flour, baking soda, ginger, cinnamon, cloves, and salt, and stir until combined. Cover with plastic wrap and chill the dough for 2 hours or overnight.

3 Heat the oven to 350°F. Line a baking sheet with parchment paper.

4 Using a spoon, scoop out dough and roll in raw sugar, turning to coat well. Transfer the dough balls to the baking sheet, spacing the cookies 1½ inches apart.

5 Bake for 10 minutes for a soft cookie, or 12 minutes for a crispy cookie. Transfer to a wire rack to cool completely.

JODIE SWEETIN'S
Peanut Butter
Kiss cookies

66 On Christmas Eve, we set out peanut butter kiss cookies for Santa. We also open up new pajamas. My mom has always done it for me, and I carry it on with my girls. **99**

ACTIVE 15 minutes / **TOTAL** 30 minutes / **MAKES** about 4 dozen cookies

INGREDIENTS

Butter for greasing the sheet
1¼ cups flour
1 tsp baking powder
¾ tsp baking soda
¼ tsp salt
½ cup butter
½ cup creamy peanut butter
½ cup sugar
½ cup brown sugar
1 egg
48 Hershey's Kisses

INSTRUCTIONS

1 Heat the oven to 375°F. Grease a cookie sheet with butter.

2 In a small bowl, whisk together the flour, baking powder, baking soda, and salt. Set aside.

3 In a large bowl, mix together the butter, peanut butter, sugar, brown sugar, and egg. Add the flour mixture and stir until a sticky dough forms.

4 Using a teaspoon, scoop out dough and roll into a ball. Place on the cookie sheet, spacing cookies 2 inches apart.

5 Bake until the cookies are golden brown, 8 to 10 minutes. While the cookies bake, unwrap the chocolates.

6 Remove the cookies from the oven and transfer to a wire rack. While the cookies are still warm, press a chocolate into the center of each cookie. Let cool completely.

CHRIS MCNALLY'S
CHOCOLATE CHIP COOKIES
WITH SEA SALT

❝ Chocolate chip cookies were always the favorite while I was growing up and are what we would leave out for Santa, along with a glass of milk and a few carrots for the reindeer! **❞**

ACTIVE 20 minutes / **TOTAL** 35 minutes / **MAKES** about 2 to 3 dozen cookies

INGREDIENTS

12 ounces semisweet chocolate bars (or whatever type of bars you like)

1 cup butter, softened

½ cup white sugar

1½ cups brown sugar

2 eggs

2 tsp vanilla extract

1 tsp baking soda

½ tsp salt

3 cups all-purpose flour

Sea salt flakes, to top, for serving

INSTRUCTIONS

1 Heat oven to 325°F. Line a baking sheet with parchment paper.

2 In a zip-top bag, add the chocolate. Using a mallet or the back of a spoon, break the chocolate into smaller pieces. Set aside.

3 In a large bowl, cream together the butter, sugar, and brown sugar until smooth. Beat in the eggs and add the vanilla.

4 In a small bowl, add 2 teaspoons hot water to the baking soda and mix until combined. Add the baking soda mixture and salt to the cookie dough. Add the flour to the cookie dough and stir until well combined. Fold in the chocolate chunks.

5 Roll into desired-size balls and place on the baking sheet. Cover a cup with plastic wrap. Use the cup to gently press each dough ball until it's shaped into a small disk. Sprinkle a pinch of sea salt flakes on each cookie.

6 Bake until the edges are golden brown, about 12 minutes. Remove from the oven and let cool.

CAMERON MATHISON'S
Sugar cookies

66 It's a tradition in my family to make our sugar cookies every year—they are my kids' favorite. And we leave them out for Santa, too! 99

ACTIVE 25 minutes / **TOTAL** 1 hour 30 minutes / **MAKES** about 5 dozen cookies

INGREDIENTS

1½ cups butter, softened

2 cups sugar

4 eggs

1 tsp vanilla extract

5 cups all-purpose flour

2 tsp baking powder

1 tsp salt

INSTRUCTIONS

1 In a large bowl, cream together the butter and sugar until smooth. Beat in the eggs and vanilla. Stir in the flour, baking powder, and salt. Cover the bowl and chill the dough at least 1 hour or overnight.

2 Heat the oven to 400°F.

3 On a lightly floured surface, roll out the dough until ¼- to ½-inch thick. With floured cookie cutters, cut the dough into as many cookies as possible. Place cookies one inch apart on ungreased cookie sheets.

4 Bake until lightly browned, about 6 to 8 minutes. Transfer the cookies to a wire rack to cool. Repeat with the remaining dough.

DECK THE PAWS

Whether on screen or curled up in our laps, furry companions underscore Christmas's unconditional love.

A HAPPY HOLIDAY

Holly Robinson Peete, who gifts her own pups a stocking full of treats and chewies each Christmas, poses with Hallmark's Happy the Dog in preparation for the Countdown to Christmas festivities.

JUST WHEN YOU THINK

HERE KITTY, KITTY

Ready-for-a-forever-home kittens roam the set of *A Very Happy & Friends Yule Log*. The three-hour program features a roaring fire, piles of presents, classical Christmas music, and precious shelter animals in an effort to promote pet rescue and adoption.

a Hallmark holiday flick can't get any more heartwarming, they go and add a furry lead to the cast. As network star Al Roker puts it, "It hardly feels like a Hallmark movie without a cute animal in the script." From Ambrose, the adorable stray tabby in *The Nine Lives of Christmas*, to the handsome horses in *Rocky Mountain Christmas*, four-legged friends bring warmth and wet-nosed charm to the films. That's especially true when pups propel the movies' storylines. Take the sweet baby hound dog Little Blade in *Debbie Macomber's Dashing Through the Snow*, who helps Ashley (Meghan Ory) and Dash (Andrew Walker) bond on an unexpected holiday road trip. There's also the now classic *A Dog Named Christmas*, where a winsome yellow Lab and a boy named Todd (Noel Fisher) rally the residents of a rural town to adopt a dog for Christmas.

The Sweet Pets

spread happiness along with the message that when you rescue an animal, you help yourself, too.

Adding to the joy are rescue pets turned network mascots Happy the Cat and Happy the Dog. Once without homes (Hallmark adopted feline Happy from an Ohio shelter; canine Happy was found on the streets of Los Angeles), they embody loyalty. The team serves as the faces of Hallmark's Adoption Ever After initiative. The program promotes pet adoption by partnering with more than 2,000 shelters across the country. To date, it has helped 70,000 pets find loving new homes. Visit *hallmarkchannel.com/adoption-ever-after* to learn more and get involved.

GET HAPPY

Aren't they fetching? Hallmark's Happy the Dog and Happy the Cat remind us that shelter animals make wonderful companions. The pair star in television specials and public events year-round to promote the adoption of rescue pets—just like them!

BEST BUDS

Actress Tamera Mowry-Housley and Hallmark resident pet expert Larissa Wohl take a puppy break on the set of *Home & Family*.

TEST YOUR CHRISTMAS IQ!
ID the movie or show for each of these photos. For the answers, see page 218.

PUPPY (AND KITTY) LOVE

In our favorite holiday movies, animals bring home the seasonal magic and love. Sometimes the pets serve as companions to a lead character who is suddenly in an unfamiliar locale. In other films, the pets full-on drive the plotline. You'll find frisky puppies unleashing mayhem, venerable dogs bringing families together just in time for the holidays, and even the occasional feline playing matchmaker. Regardless of their screen time, these loyal furry friends supply comfort and joy.

MAN'S BEST FRIEND

Like a scruffy beard or a rugged puffer coat, the on-screen pets of Hallmark's leading men often give us a glimpse into the hearts of the characters. Whether it's a prized horse that puts a prince at ease or a pesky cat that reveals the soft side of a confirmed bachelor, the animals help convey the true feelings of the characters with a mere nuzzle or snuggle. They also have a way of getting even the staunchest Scrooge into the Christmas spirit. If a picture can paint a thousand words, then an on-screen animal companion just may paint ten thousand—most of them festive!

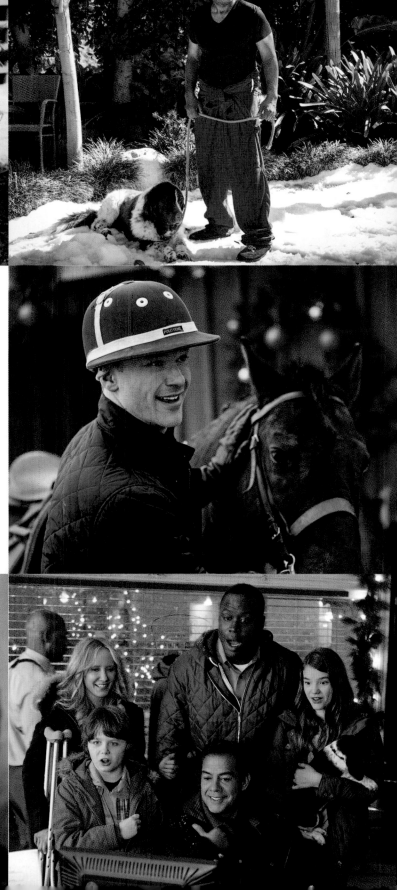

Turning a Pet into a Star

Sarah Clifford, Hallmark's head animal trainer,
shares the ins and outs of training furry friends to appear on film.

Q: Dogs and cats are universally adorable. How do you determine if a particular animal is suited for the movies?

A: It all comes down to personality. I look for traits such as friendly to strangers, outgoing in nature, confident, playful with toys, treat-motivated, nonreactive to new noises, able to tolerate different sounds, and tolerant of other animals. A unique look never hurts, either!

Q: What is a day on the set like for animal talent?

A: It is generally like a day for human talent! There is rehearsal time and then filming. We re-create the scenes as closely as possible before we arrive on set so there is some familiarity. Between takes, the dogs and cats have comfy beds, toys, treats, and a quiet place to rest. The cast and crew are always very sweet and accommodating to the animals as well.

Q: Working with animals must bring challenges. What's one of the most common?

A: For the holiday films, the most frequent animal-meets-filming challenge is snow. Fake snow can prove tricky because many types require us to wash the animals' paws between takes. When it's real snow, the cold temperatures will sometimes throw them off. But the animals ultimately love playing, and performing, in it.

ANIMAL HOUSE During the annual *A Very Happy & Friends Yule Log*, Happy the Dog and Happy the Cat hold court with a darling menagerie of ready-to-be-rescued animals. While cute puppies and kitties receive the majority of the screen time, sweet bunnies, ducks, and other farm critters also make their appearances. Pipsqueak the Pig is a perennial favorite.

BOUGHS OF JOLLY

Trim your tree with treasured ornaments that recall happy family memories and plenty of good cheer.

Create

EASY ORNAMENTS

1. SPARKLING BULBS

Turn old night-light bulbs into festive Christmas ornaments. Just brush on glittering glue, roll the bulb in glitter, and let dry for 15 minutes. Then hot-glue a loop of metallic embroidery floss to the bulb's base.

2. PRETTY PAPER SHIELDS

Glue wrapping paper to one side of cardstock. Create a shield-shaped template; place on the paper-covered card. Trace the template and cut out the shape. Use a hole punch to make a hole in the top; hang with a piece of rickrack.

3. RIBBON "CANDY"

Fold a length of striped ribbon into loops as shown and pass a needle threaded with strong cotton thread through its center, adding a stack of buttons at both ends. Tie knots to secure, then create a loop of thread for hanging.

4. PATCHWORK ORBS

Cover a Styrofoam ball with scraps of coordinating fabric, using the dull edge of a knife to press in the edges. Continue until everything is tucked in, then sew on a loop of twine to hang.

"

My personal favorite ornament is the Hallmark Keepsake Butterfly. I always say that my mom visits me in the form of butterflies. I unveiled that ornament my first day co-hosting *Home & Family* and it immediately put me at ease. I knew my mom was with me and telling me to relax.

—LARISSA WOHL, HALLMARK *HOME & FAMILY* PET EXPERT

"

SMALL WONDERS
Paint a classic Scandi pattern or turn your kids loose with markers for a fun and festive art project.

Create
DALA CLAY HORSES

Dala horses are a staple in Swedish folk art. Considered good luck charms, they often grace Christmas trees. To make your own, start with white oven-bake clay, an old rolling pin, and a Dala horse–shaped cookie cutter.

• Roll out one sheet of clay evenly to $\frac{3}{16}$-inch thick (any less and the decorations will be too fragile and break).

• Cut out horses using the cookie cutter. Press excess clay together and roll it out again to make more. Repeat as needed.

• Determine where the hole for the ribbon should be on each horse. (Hold each horse between your fingertips to simulate it hanging from a ribbon to ensure each one will hang level.)

• Using a knitting needle or wooden skewer, make a hole ¼ inch from the edge, moving the needle in a circular motion to make the hole big enough.

• Following package instructions, bake the clay.

• When the decorations have hardened, tidy up any rough edges with a craft knife.

• Using watered-down red acrylic paint, paint your designs. When dry, do the same on the reverse side.

O CHRISTMAS TREE!
STAR SELECTS

66 Now that my kids are all grown up and we don't have to keep *all* the homemade ornaments they made in kindergarten (hehe), my approach is to have a beautiful tree that matches the theme and colors of our warm and modern beach home. 99

—CANDACE CAMERON BURE

66 I love this ornament, because I love the red pickup truck from the *Christmas in Evergreen* movies. It is such a beautiful classic American truck and reminds me so much of my home state of Virginia. 99

—DEBBIE MATENOPOULOS

CHAPTER 4

Create A Happy Ending

LOVE IS IN THE AIR

Here's to the on-screen romances that set us aglow each season.

MEMORY MAKER

In *Memories of Christmas*, Dave (Mark Taylor) and Noelle (Christina Milian) are at odds—until he brings her over to the merry side.

CHRISTMAS AND ROMANCE MAKE A PERFECT PAIR.

With lights twinkling, fires roaring, and snow falling, it's only natural that love would be in the air. Maybe that's why at the heart of almost every Hallmark holiday flick is an intoxicating love story.

"Romance is defined as a feeling of excitement and mystery associated with love. Sounds a lot like Christmas, doesn't it?" says frequent network director Jonathan Wright, whose films include *Angel Falls: A Novel Holiday*, *Christmas Next Door*, and *A Very Merry Mix-Up*. (No wonder so many of us like to snuggle up under a cozy blanket and watch the movies with our sweetie by our side!)

CHANGE OF HEART

In *Romance at Reindeer Lodge*, Molly (Nicky Whelan) settles for snow instead of sand when she accidentally ends up on a flight to Vermont instead of Jamaica. After she meets Jared (Josh Kelly), her discontent melts away.

HAVING A BALL

For their roles in *A Majestic Christmas*, Jerrika Hinton and Christian Vincent filmed scenes together ice skating, tangoing on Main Street, and building a snowman. The latter resulted in an on-screen snowball fight.

KICKING OFF EVERY LOVE STORY

is a meet-cute. That's the film term used to describe the amusing first encounter that leads to the development of a romantic relationship. With attractive strangers accidentally spilling coffee onto one another or knocking over Christmas ornaments, these meet-cutes have a sweetness and everyday charm that tugs at our heartstrings. "We take our meet-cutes very seriously around here," says writer Tracy Andreen, who has worked on more than 20 movies for the network. "They play out so effortlessly on screen, because we search for that natural motivation for them to occur. Then we just let them happen. They feel satisfyingly real because, in a sense, they are."

WHEN IN ROME

"Rome isn't about what you see. It's about how it makes you feel." Lacey Chabert's favorite quote from her film *Christmas in Rome* also applies to the relationship between her character, Angela, and nuisance-turned-budding-love-interest Oliver (Sam Page).

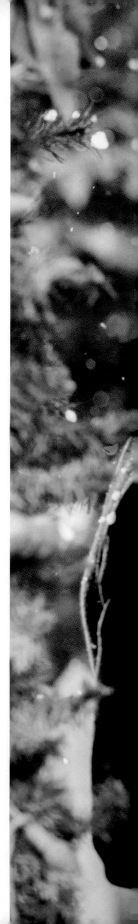

WHEN GIRL MEETS BOY

on screen or in real life, fireworks don't always spark. Falling in love means slowly discovering what you adore about each other.

The lighthearted introductions are just the start of the fun. We watch as the pair overcome obstacles; in *A Majestic Christmas*, for instance, architect Nell (Jarrika Hinton) and real estate developer Connor (Christian Vincent) clash over their vision for a historic theater. Slowly, they fall for each other. And let's face it: It's not hard to fall for these leading men. Handsome, wholesome, witty—each great guy is an upright citizen who appreciates an independent-minded woman. It's easy to get swept off your feet.

But the story is about so much more than the magnetism of these hunky love interests. We are drawn to the heroine's moral compass, which sees her through a journey of maturing into her full self and answering the hard questions of who she really is.

DESTINATION LOVE

"Every Hallmark movie needs snow! Lots and lots of snow!" says Candace Cameron Bure, shown here with Paul Greene in *A Christmas Detour*.

TEST YOUR CHRISTMAS IQ!
Can you ID the movies that feature these weddings? For the answers, see page 219.

MERRY ME

"Joy to the world" takes on new meaning when a film features Christmassy nuptials. But that's merely the icing on the (wedding) cake. These on-screen unions aren't just fabulous fetes. They celebrate the best of what marriage can be—two equals coming together to bring out the best in each other. Here's to adding some happily-ever-after to the happiest season of all!

FROM SMALL MOMENTS

to big milestones, these movies remind us
of our own cherished love stories.

MAGIC MOMENT

In *Engaging Father Christmas*, the second installment of the *Finding Father Christmas* franchise, Miranda (Erin Krakow) and Ian (Niall Matter) cap off an idyllic horse-drawn carriage ride, fittingly led by a colt named Prancer, with a picture-perfect engagement under the small-town gazebo.

The budding on-screen romances are all the more satisfying when they play out across multiple holiday movies. In the *Finding Father Christmas* franchise, for example, we follow characters Miranda (Erin Krakow) and Ian (Niall Matter) across three films, from their initial encounter to their magical engagement to their joyous nuptials, complete with a dreamy Christmas Eve wedding.

And, oh, the weddings. Hallmark films play host to numerous nuptials, each one as decidedly picturesque as the one before. While we all love to see a couple's big day, Andreen points out that they're not the ultimate endgame for our heroines: "It's never just about that. It's definitely a reward, but not the sole goal in her arc. Whether she's saving a small-town business or discovering her family's past, they emphasize strength and self-improvement at all times."

SAY YES!

Jodie Sweetin kept her fingers crossed for a role in a Hallmark film. The timing finally worked with *Finding Santa*, which concludes with her character, Grace, receiving a proposal from Ben (Eric Winter)—and resounding approval from onlooking family and friends.

FAITH IN HUMANITY

In their own special way, each film reminds us that people are inherently kind, and communities rally together when it matters most.

Those happy endings rooted in the heroine's determination, inner strength, and warmth are what keep us coming back for more (sometimes on repeat during a pajama-clad, movie-bingeing Saturday in December). "Life is hard and scary, and love in the real world makes people crazy sometimes," points out Andreen. "Hallmark stories remind us that people are generally good, kindness is a virtue to be rewarded, and falling in love can lead to something wonderful. They act as a welcome balm for the heart and soul."

SWEATER WEATHER

Holly (Brooke D'Orsay) and Sam (Marc Blucas) bond over a tacky sweater tradition in *Miss Christmas*. "It's cool to play someone so full of life. She reminds me of that better part of myself," says D'Orsay.

166

A SWEET CONNECTION

In *A Christmas Duet*, former flames and ex-music partners Averie (Chaley Rose) and Jesse (Rome Flynn) reconnect at her Vermont lodge over the holidays—and rediscover their all-star chemistry.

CRAFTING A LOVE STORY

Veteran Hallmark screenwriter Tracy Andreen reveals the must-haves for writing an irresistible romance, from that first encounter to the heartwarming ending.

Q: What do all Hallmark screenplays need for that signature sparkle?

A: Emotion, fun, but mainly honesty. Audiences are smart—they'll stop caring and connecting almost immediately if they sense that the moments aren't genuine. So I always find the honesty in the characters' emotions and exchanges— even the goofy ones—and then let everything flow from that point.

Q: Why is Christmas the ultimate backdrop for romantic comedies?

A: The wonderful thing about holiday movies is that the audience is already primed to give in to their emotions. Tradition, nostalgia, even end-of-the-year exhaustion create a sort of shorthand between the storytellers and the viewers. They are ready to wear their heart on their sleeve and eager to watch characters who do the same.

Q: Nobody can resist a love story with a happy ending. What else keeps us coming back?

A: Sure, everyone is here for the romance. But there's a strong focus on both the female and male leads. It is important to make sure they both have clear internal arcs that show how each of them grows stronger from meeting each other. There is no settling or sacrificing to be had for either party!

DYNAMIC DUOS You won't catch a leading couple going on a ho-hum dinner date. Courtship means rolling up your sleeves and getting active—whether skating, baking, making music, or tossing snowballs. More often than not, the pair's love grows as they share their joy with friends, family, and neighbors.

TEST YOUR CHRISTMAS IQ!
Guess these Christmas movies and the actors and actresses who star in them. For the answers, turn to page 219.

SWEET FINISHES

Cap your special meal with a delicious dessert, plus warming hot drinks to sip in front of a roaring fire.

LACEY CHABERT'S
Sweet Potato Pie with Homemade Whipped Cream

" My grandfather made this pie every Christmas. It's so delicious. You weren't allowed to pass through the kitchen without trying it! Every time I bake it, I think of all the good memories spending Christmas at my grandparents' house. **"**

ACTIVE 30 minutes / **TOTAL** 1 hour 30 minutes / **MAKES** 10 servings

INGREDIENTS

- 1 prepared pie crust
- 1 stick butter, melted
- 2 cups sugar
- 2 eggs
- 2 heaping Tbsp flour
- 1 cup mashed white sweet potato
- 2 tsp vanilla
-   Pinch of salt

WHIPPED CREAM

- 2 cups heavy cream
- 2 Tbsp confectioners' sugar

INSTRUCTIONS

1 Heat the oven to 350°F. Unroll pie crust and fit into the bottom and up the side of a pie plate; crimp as desired.

2 In a large bowl, mix butter, sugar, and eggs until creamy. Add flour, sweet potato, vanilla, and salt; stir to combine.

3 Pour the sweet potato filling into the prepared pie crust and bake until just set but still slightly wobbly in the center, 45 to 50 minutes.

4 While the pie bakes, prepare the whipped cream. In a chilled bowl, pour in the heavy cream. Gradually add the confectioners' sugar, mixing with a hand mixer on medium speed until soft peaks form. Set aside.

5 Remove the pie from the oven and let cool completely. Top with whipped cream and serve.

LEMON-BUTTERMILK TART

"I'm not the best in the kitchen, but if someone else is doing the baking, I don't discriminate. I love any dessert with fruit in it."
—Kellie Pickler

ACTIVE 25 minutes / **TOTAL** 4 hours 10 minutes / **MAKES** 8 servings

INGREDIENTS

2 ½ cups all-purpose flour, spooned and leveled

1 tsp Kosher salt

1 tsp sugar

1 cup cold unsalted butter, cut up

¼ cup ice water

PIE FILLING

1 Tbsp all-purpose flour

⅔ cup buttermilk

½ cup sugar

2 Tbsp light brown sugar

2 large eggs

2 tsp finely grated lemon zest, plus ¼ cup lemon juice

2 Tbsp unsalted butter, melted

⅛ tsp Kosher salt

Confectioners' sugar, for dusting

INSTRUCTIONS

1 Whisk together the flour, salt, and sugar. Cut in the butter until it resembles coarse meal with several pea-size pieces remaining. Add water, 1 tablespoon at a time, using a fork to pull the dough together into a crumbly pile (add up to an additional 2 tablespoons of water if needed).

2 Divide the dough into two piles; wrap each in plastic wrap. Use the plastic to flatten and press the dough into disks. Refrigerate until firm, 2 hours.

3 Heat the oven to 350°F. On a floured surface, roll one dough disk into an 11-inch circle. (Reserve the second disk for later use.) Transfer the dough to a 9-inch tart pan with a removable bottom. Press the dough into the corners; fold the overhang into the pan and press firmly into flutes. Freeze for 15 minutes.

4 Cover the chilled dough with parchment paper, leaving an overhang, and fill with dried beans. On a rimmed baking sheet, bake the crust until the edges are golden brown, 30 to 35 minutes. Remove the parchment and beans. Bake until the bottom is light golden and dry, 5 to 10 minutes.

5 Make the filling: Whisk together the flour, buttermilk, sugar, brown sugar, eggs, lemon zest, lemon juice, butter, and salt. Carefully pour into the warm tart crust to within ¼ inch of the top. Bake until the filling is set, 50 to 60 minutes. Cool on a rack for at least 2 hours.

6 Remove the tart ring and dust with confectioners' sugar.

KEN WINGARD'S
RUSSIAN TEA CAKES

" These are easy to make. The kids like rolling them in the powdered sugar (plenty of finger licking is involved), but they always end up looking surprisingly elegant. **"**

ACTIVE 20 minutes / **TOTAL** 60 minutes / **MAKES** about 2½ dozen cookies

INGREDIENTS

- 1 cup butter, softened
- ½ cup confectioners' sugar, plus more for dusting baked cookies
- 1 tsp vanilla
- 1¾ cups all-purpose flour, plus more for dusting hands
- 1 cup pecans, finely chopped (optional)

INSTRUCTIONS

1 Heat the oven to 275°F.

2 In a large bowl, cream the butter and sugar together until smooth. Beat in the vanilla. Stir in the flour, combining until dough forms. Fold in the pecans, if using.

3 Scoop about 1 tablespoon of dough. With floured hands, shape it into a ball. Continue to dust your hands with a little flour as you make more cookies. Place the cookies about one inch apart on an ungreased baking sheet.

4 Bake until golden brown, about 40 minutes. Remove the cookies from the oven and leave on the baking sheet until cool enough to handle.

5 Roll the warm cookies in additional confectioners' sugar. Place on a wire rack to cool completely.

HOT CHOCOLATE

Fun fact: Hallmark Christmas movies have featured an amazing 279,825 gallons of hot cocoa! Here's how to mix your own comforting cup—topped with whipped cream, naturally.

ACTIVE 10 minutes / **TOTAL** 15 minutes / **MAKES** 4 to 6 servings

INGREDIENTS

- 1 cup heavy cream
- 2 Tbsp confectioners' sugar
- 2 tsp vanilla extract
- 6 ounces semisweet chocolate, chopped
- 1⅔ cups boiling water
- 1½ cups whole milk

  Unsweetened cocoa powder, for serving (optional)

INSTRUCTIONS

1 In a small bowl, with a mixer on medium speed, beat the cream with the confectioners' sugar and vanilla until stiff peaks form. Cover and refrigerate until needed.

2 Place the chocolate in a 1-quart saucepan. Pour ⅓ cup of the boiling water over the chocolate and stir until the chocolate melts. Whisk in the milk and remaining 1⅓ cups boiling water; cook over medium heat until hot but not boiling, whisking constantly.

3 Ladle the hot chocolate into mugs and dollop with the chilled whipped cream. Sprinkle with cocoa powder, if desired, and serve.

Every Hallmark Christmas
Script Needs...
Hot cocoa and lots of
twinkly lights!
—DANICA MCKELLAR

DANICA MCKELLAR'S
CHOCOLATE YULE LOG

*❝ Around the holidays I love to make—and eat—my mom's chocolate Yule log.
My favorite part (aside from how it tastes!) is decorating it with my son.
We love to mold the little snowmen, holly leaves, and candy canes from marzipan
and then paint them with food coloring. ❞*

ACTIVE 45 minutes / **TOTAL** 1 hour / **MAKES** 12 servings

INGREDIENTS

Ghee, butter, or coconut oil for greasing pan

6 organic eggs, separated

¾ cup organic cane sugar, divided

⅓ cup organic unsweetened cocoa powder

2 tsp organic pure vanilla extract

⅓ tsp (a small pinch) pure sea salt

Organic confectioners' sugar

VANILLA CREAM FILLING

¾ cup organic heavy/whipping cream

¼ cup organic confectioners' sugar

½ tsp organic pure vanilla extract

CHOCOLATE CREAM TOPPING

1¼ cups organic heavy/whipping cream

⅓ cup + 1 Tbsp organic confectioners' sugar

3½ Tbsp organic unsweetened cocoa powder

1 tsp organic pure vanilla extract

DECORATIONS

Marzipan

Red and green food coloring

Small watercolor paint brushes

INSTRUCTIONS

1 Heat the oven to 375°F. Use ghee, butter, or coconut oil to lightly grease a 10-by-15-inch jelly roll baking pan. Line the bottom of the pan with unbleached parchment and then very lightly grease the paper.

2 Place the egg whites in the bowl of a stand mixer. (Make sure no yolk is mixed in with your egg whites.) At high speed, beat the egg whites until soft peaks form. Add ¼ cup of the sugar, 2 tablespoons at a time, beating well after each addition, and then continue to beat just until stiff peaks form. (Careful: Overbeating will make the meringue not hold its shape, and the cake will be heavy.) Set aside.

3 In another mixing bowl, use the stand mixer to beat the egg yolks at high speed, adding the remaining ½ cup sugar, 2 tablespoons at a time, beating until the mixture is very thick, about 3 to 5 minutes.

4 At low speed, stir in the cocoa powder, vanilla extract, and sea salt. Mix just until smooth.

5 With a large spoon or rubber spatula, gently fold the cocoa mixture and egg whites together until just

CONTINUED ON PAGE 184

CONTINUED FROM PAGE 182

blended and no egg whites show. Pour the batter into the prepared baking pan and use a spatula to spread evenly.

6 Bake until the surface springs back when gently pressed with a fingertip, 12 to 15 minutes. Do not overbake or the cake will crack instead of roll.

7 Sift a tiny amount of confectioners' sugar onto one side of a thin, clean dish towel, at least 10 by 15 inches in size. When you take the cake out of the oven, carefully turn it out onto the sugared towel. Lift the pan off the cake, then peel away the parchment paper and discard.

8 Roll the cake up, rolling the towel as well, into a jelly roll, starting at the shorter side if you want a fatter log, or starting at the longer side if you want a thinner log. Cool the rolled cake completely on a rack, seam side down.

ASSEMBLE THE YULE LOG

1 Make the vanilla cream filling: In a medium bowl, combine the heavy cream, confectioners' sugar, and vanilla extract. Beat until thick. Cream whips up best if it is chilled, just out of the refrigerator. Also, watch out: Overbeating cream will turn it into butter. If not using immediately, cover and chill until ready to use.

2 Make the chocolate cream topping: In a medium-large bowl, combine the heavy cream, confectioners' sugar, cocoa powder, and vanilla. Beat until thick. (If not using immediately, cover and chill until ready to use.)

3 Carefully unroll the cake, removing the towel as you do so. Spread all of the vanilla cream filling evenly across the top of the cake up to ½ inch from the edges. Reroll the cake and place it seam side down on a serving plate.

4 Cover the top, sides, and ends of the log with the chocolate cream topping. (To keep the serving plate clean, slide waxed paper around the edges of the cake and then carefully remove it when you're finished putting the topping on.) Using a fork or small spatula, make slightly wavy lines in the chocolate cream on the top and sides of the cake to create a bark effect. Use a spatula to make a swirl on each end of the cake to give the look of a cut log.

5 Loosely cover the cake in foil, 12 to 15 minutes, and refrigerate for at least 1 hour before serving it. Take the cake out about 30 minutes before serving, as the taste and texture are best at room temperature.

DECORATE AND SERVE

1 Mold the marzipan to create 2 holly clusters, each with 2 holly leaves joined with 3 or more holly berries. Use food coloring to paint the leaves green and berries red. Allow to dry completely.

2 Before serving, if you want a snowy look, lightly sift confectioners' sugar over the log and plate. Decorate with the marzipan holly leaves. You can space them out on top of the log or put one cluster on the log and the other at the base of it.

3 After serving, return the cake to the refrigerator so your filling and topping don't spoil. This cake will still be delicious up to 3 days later if you keep it chilled—and it hasn't been completely eaten by then!

THAT'S A WRAP

Take your gift giving up a notch. Crafty packaging ideas
make each present feel like one of a kind.

TRUE COLORS

Whether you opt for classic red, green, and gold or pick other patterns and colors, wrapping presents in a cohesive palette makes for a pretty under-the-tree display.

Wrap It With
TREAT BAGS

Don't toss those too-small-to-cover-a-gift-box pieces of wrapping paper! Instead, transform them into pretty packaging for small goodies and gift cards.

To make: Begin by cutting a rectangle of paper that's large enough to cover both sides of the item, plus a little extra. (An inch of overage should be sufficient.) With the paper wrong side up, fold over a ½-inch flap on the long bottom edge. Next, fold the two short edges of the rectangle. Fold the paper in half along its longer side, wrong sides together, then use double-sided tape to adhere the flaps along the bottom and the side opposite the fold. This will leave only the top of the envelope open. Fold over ¾ inch at the top and cut the corners at an angle to make the envelope-style flap. Seal with a small sticker (left) or use a grommet tool (right) to create a hole to thread twine through.
Tip: When gifting baked treats, wrap them in parchment before inserting into envelopes.

1. CROWD-PLEASERS
Share the love with mail carriers, teachers, and other special helpers by handing out festive thank-you gifts of holiday sweets.

2. STAMP IT OUT
Simple stamps and stencils give "scrappy" packages a sophisticated finish. Use them to write recipients' names in lieu of gift tags.

189

Wrap It With

UNEXPECTED GIFT TOPPERS

What completes a thoughtful present that was so clearly chosen with the recipient in mind? A playful presentation! Here, four clever ideas for showstopping finishing touches.

①

A metallic pom-pom placed off-kilter.

②

A plucked-from-the-yard evergreen sprig with twine.

③

Super-fluffy yarn straight out of the craft bin.

4

Flags made from party straws and wire-edged ribbon
tucked under constrasting rickrack and ribbon.

Spread the Love

A GRATITUDE LETTER

Hallmark characters always take a moment to count their blessings.
Make a point to do the same by writing a note of thanks this holiday season.

One true highlight of the season is cherishing and toasting our closest friends and family members. But it's also a wonderful time to recognize someone outside our immediate circle. Sharing appreciation for a person we feel indebted to but have never properly thanked is a gift for both the giver and recipient. Why write a gratitude letter? Research shows that people who express gratitude are happier, possibly because it shifts the focus from what isn't perfect in our world to the many blessings we do have.

   To get started, ask yourself: Who is someone I deeply admire and would like to give props to? It could be your high school soccer coach, a career mentor, a helpful neighbor, that cousin who doubles as family photographer—anyone deserving praise.

   It's always great to be as specific as possible about what you appreciate. So instead of writing to a hospice nurse, "Thank you for helping my father," you might share something like, "Your kindness and sense of calm helped our whole family feel more at peace."

   You can also praise something minor that meant the world to you. A note to a childhood friend's mom might read, "I still think about the delicious curries you cooked. You opened my eyes (and my taste buds!) to a wider world."

   Your final step: Drop that card or letter in the postbox. And don't be surprised if you get a happy note back. Gratitude cards tend to be contagious—in a great way. Receiving one makes you want to grab a pen and paper and thank someone special, too.

"

I love nothing more than
seeing the holidays through
my children's eyes.

—TAMERA MOWRY-HOUSLEY

"

"

I love hearing the voices of my
friends and family. It makes me
grateful to have that support.

—STEPHEN HUSZAR

"

"

I am most grateful to have
family together, to be healthy,
and to live in what is still the
greatest country in the world.

—AL ROKER

"

"

Christmas cards are one of my
highlights of the year. It's not
just an updated family photo, but
highlights of what we've been
grateful for during the year.

—CANDACE CAMERON BURE

"

"

Before Christmas dinner we all
say something we're thankful
for (the kids say something
adorable!), then my dad leads
us in a blessing over the food.

—LACEY CHABERT

"

CHAPTER 5

CHEERS
TO GREAT
FRIENDS

FaLaLaLa A FUN

From games to tunes, these party plans will
inspire revelry befitting a scene right out of a movie.
(Inviting the whole town is encouraged!)

CARRIED AWAY

Debbie Matenopoulos and Nick Lachey sport over-the-top Christmas sweaters. Invite party guests to do the same to get into the holiday swing of things.

Watch & Play

MOVIE BINGO

Turn viewing into hands-on fun. Use this card as inspiration to make your party bingo cards.
Set out peppermint candies for Christmassy game markers!

Handsome Man Saves Someone Mid-Fall	A Christmas Tree Lot Figures into the Plot	Big City Career Gal Reluctantly Returns to Hometown	Look! We're Ice Skating!	A Furry Friend Steals the Show
Charming Local Café	Impromptu Snowman-Building Session	Santa Makes a Holiday Wish Come True	Winter Weather Thwarts Travel Plans	Someone Exclaims, "I'd Forgotten How Fun This Is!"
Neighbor Hosts a Cookie Swap	Wedding Where the Whole Town Is Invited	FREE SPACE	Friendly Winter Competition Between Potential Love Interests	Two or More Characters Sing a Christmas Carol
Impending Threat of a Family Business Going Under	Sips Hot Cocoa. Has Whipped Cream on Nose	Male Character Wearing a Cozy Sweater	Cameo by a Famous Singer	Time to Decorate the Tree!
A Wise Aunt or Uncle Says Just the Right Thing	Leading Lady Rallies Town to Save Christmas	Sparks Fly in Front of a Cozy Fire	Female Character Has a Creative Career	Someone Unexpectedly Bumps into an Ex

View Finder

GIRLS' NIGHT IN!

Did you know that from October through December, Hallmark airs nearly 5,000 hours of holiday magic? Here are top picks to view with your crew. Count how many you've seen.

1. Merry & Bright Cate (Jodie Sweetin) and Gabe (Andrew Walker) join forces to save a candy cane company.

2. The Sweetest Christmas A struggling pastry chef (Lacey Chabert) finally embraces the true spirit of the holidays.

3. Memories of Christmas Noelle (Christina Milian) meets her match in Dave (Mark Taylor) in her hometown.

4. A Christmas Miracle Magazine editor Emma (Tamera Mowry-Housley) finds love with Marcus (Brooks Darnell).

5. A Family Christmas Gift Amber (Holly Robinson Peete) visits the inn of her aunt (Patti LaBelle) and saves the day.

6. Christmas Town In Grandon Falls, Lauren (Candace Cameron Bure) discovers love, family, and Christmas.

7. Christmas at Graceland Laurel (Kellie Pickler) is asked by her ex to perform at the Graceland Christmas Concert.

8. Christmas at Grand Valley Artist Kelly (Danica McKellar) goes back to Grand Valley. Will she open her heart?

HOLLY, JOLLY MUSIC

These holiday tunes and traditions put Hallmark stars in a merry state of mind.

"
My favorite way to get into the spirit? Christmas music! Give me Bing Crosby and Mariah Carey, and I'm *in it*.

—CANDACE CAMERON BURE
"

"
We are usually overseas entertaining military families and service members for the holidays. I wouldn't have it any other way!

—KELLIE PICKLER
"

"
Play 'Sleigh Ride' or 'God Rest Ye Merry Gentlemen' and I'm instantly in the spirit. My list also includes Dolly Parton and Elvis Presley.

—DANICA MCKELLAR
"

"
Listening to Christmas music and relaxing in front of a fire always does the trick to get me in the holiday mood.

—HOLLY ROBINSON PEETE
"

All I want for Christmas is...

no one to interrupt my Hallmark holiday movies.

KEEP CALM AND HALLMARK ON

Bake cookies. Wrap presents. *Watch Hallmark movies.* Repeat.

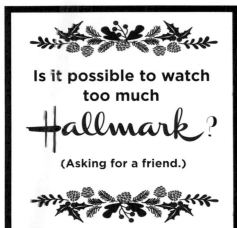

Is it possible to watch too much Hallmark?

(Asking for a friend.)

Team Meme
SHARE THE JOY

Snap photos of the phrases that resonate and share using #CountdownToChristmas.

If Hallmark bingeing is wrong, I don't want to be right.

Happy the Dog is my (virtual) pet

Hallmark on T.V. Hot cocoa in hand. Today is going to be epic.

Eat, Drink & Be Merry

(And by merry, I mean watch Hallmark movies nonstop.)

THE HALLMARK MOVIE CHALLENGE

Think you know your Christmas films inside and out? Put that knowledge to the test! Play with your guests to see who binge-watches (and knows the stars) best. A little friendly competition never hurt anyone! Find the answers on page 219.

1. ANDREW WALKER PLAYED TWO OF THESE PROFESSIONS IN HALLMARK HOLIDAY FILMS. WHICH ONE HAS HE NOT PLAYED? (YET!)

a) Undercover agent

b) Baseball player

c) Antarctic explorer

3. WHICH HALLMARK STAR WAS BORN IN GERMANY?

a) Alicia Witt

b) Tia Mowry-Hardrict

c) Kellie Pickler

2. WHICH TRADITIONAL DISH DO ALEXA AND CARLOS PENAVEGA MAKE FOR CHRISTMAS DINNER?

a) Sancocho stew

b) Bouillabaisse

c) Paella

4. LACEY CHABERT HAS HAD MANY INTERESTING CAREERS IN HER HALLMARK CHRISTMAS MOVIE ROLES. WHICH OF THESE IS NOT ONE OF THEM?

a) Zookeeper

b) Gingerbread baker

c) Wildlife reserve owner

5. WHAT DOES DANICA MCKELLAR BAKE FOR DESSERT EVERY CHRISTMAS?

a) A white coconut cake

b) A chocolate Yule log

c) A pear tart

6. WHICH OF THESE PLACES IS NOT THE LOCATION OF A HALLMARK CHRISTMAS MOVIE?

a) Burnaby, British Columbia

b) Grand Ole Opry, Tennessee

c) Santa Claus, Indiana

7. WHICH ACTRESS NURSED A REINDEER BACK TO HEALTH? (ON SCREEN, THAT IS!)

a) Holly Robinson Peete

b) Candace Cameron Bure

c) Alicia Witt

8. HOW DID HAPPY THE CAT GET DISCOVERED?

a) He was repped by an elite animal talent agency

b) He was rescued from an Ohio animal shelter

c) He was wandering the streets of Los Angeles

9. IN THE MOVIE *A BOYFRIEND FOR CHRISTMAS*, SANTA...

a) Falls in love with Holly (Kelli Williams)

b) Breaks up with Holly

c) Plays matchmaker for Holly

10. WHICH CANINE IS A HALLMARK CHANNEL FAVORITE?

a) Happy the Dog

b) Lucky the Dog

c) Santa's Little Helper

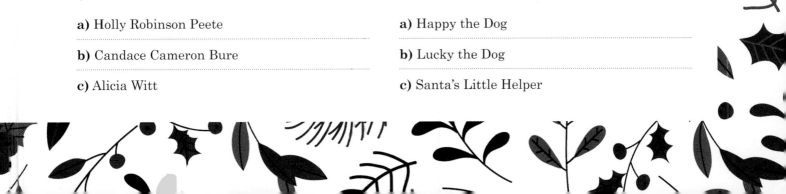

EAT, DRINK & BE MERRY

Elevate your party spread with fun drinks
and delicious nibbles.

A NIGHT TO REMEMBER

Love blooms when event planner Mia (Adelaide Kane) taps her brother's friend David (Carlos PenaVega) to help her pull off a VIP party in *A Midnight Kiss.*

DEBBIE MATENOPOULOS'S
MAPLE ROSEMARY POPCORN

❝ I love movie night with an amped-up snack of maple rosemary popcorn.
It is delectable—like a fancy kettle corn. ❞

ACTIVE 10 minutes / **TOTAL** 15 minutes / **MAKES** 6 to 8 servings

INGREDIENTS

- 1 cup popcorn kernels
- 3 Tbsp grapeseed oil
- ¼ cup butter
- 4 sprigs rosemary
- 5 Tbsp maple sugar
- 1 Tbsp confectioners' sugar
- 1 tsp Kosher salt
- ¼ tsp black pepper

INSTRUCTIONS

1 Pour the popcorn kernels and oil into the bottom of a large stockpot. Cover the pot with a lid and put it over high heat.

2 When you hear the first few kernels popping, grab the pot and gently shake it back and forth over the heat (about 3 to 4 inches above the burner). This keeps the corn from burning.

3 When you hear about 2 seconds of silence between popping sounds, you know you've popped nearly every kernel. Turn off the heat and carefully remove the lid. Pour the popped corn into a large mixing bowl.

4 Melt the butter in a sauté pan and toss in the rosemary sprigs. Cook the rosemary until it crisps up; shut off the heat before the butter browns.

5 Add the maple sugar, confectioners' sugar, salt, and pepper to a spice grinder and pulse until evenly combined. Pour the spice mixture over the popped corn. Toss with your hands a few times to combine.

6 Drizzle the melted butter on top and continue stirring with your hands (or tongs) until the popcorn is uniformly coated.

HOLLY ROBINSON PEETE'S
MACARONI AND CHEESE

❝ My favorite recipe is Patti LaBelle's mac and cheese. I usually make it around the holidays. It's so delicious because Patti uses five cheeses! ❞

ACTIVE 30 minutes / **TOTAL** 1 hour / **MAKES** 8 servings

INGREDIENTS

Butter for greasing the dish

1 pound macaroni

1 Tbsp vegetable oil

8 Tbsp butter

½ cup Muenster cheese, shredded

½ cup mild cheddar cheese, shredded

½ cup sharp cheddar cheese, shredded

½ cup Monterey Jack cheese, shredded

2 cups half-and-half

8 ounces Velveeta cheese, cubed

2 eggs, lightly beaten

¼ tsp seasoning salt

⅛ tsp freshly ground pepper

1 Tbsp butter

INSTRUCTIONS

1 Heat the oven to 350°F. Grease a 2½-quart baking dish with butter. Set aside.

2 In a large pot, add water and bring to a boil over high heat. Add macaroni and oil. Cook according to macaroni package instructions. Drain over a colander and return macaroni to pot.

3 In a small saucepan, melt 8 tablespoons butter. Pour the melted butter over the macaroni and stir to combine.

4 In a large bowl, combine shredded cheeses. Add 1½ cups of the shredded cheeses, half-and-half, cubed cheese, and eggs to the macaroni. Season to taste with salt and pepper.

5 Transfer the macaroni to the prepared baking dish; top with remaining ½ cup cheese. Dot with remaining 1 tablespoon butter. Bake until edges are golden brown and bubbly, about 30 to 35 minutes. Remove from the oven and let cool for 15 minutes before serving.

Twelve Crostini

Expecting a full house? You can't go wrong with a mash-up of baguette plus toppings. Set out a few (or all!) of these crostini variations and don't be surprised if they disappear fast.

ACTIVE PER CROSTINI 5 to 10 minutes / **TOTAL** 10 to 20 minutes / **MAKES** 16 crostini per recipe

1. Blueberry & Jalapeño
Combine ⅔ cup ricotta, 1 chopped scallion, and Kosher salt. Top 16 toasted baguette slices with the ricotta mixture, 3 Tbsp blueberry jam, and jalapeño slices.

2. Beet Hummus & Chickpea
In a food processor, combine 15½ ounces chickpeas, 1 cooked beet, ¼ cup olive oil, 3 Tbsp mint, 2 garlic cloves, 1 Tbsp lemon juice, ¾ tsp ground cumin, and salt. Top 16 toasted baguette slices with the hummus; garnish with chickpeas and mint.

3. Pickled Shallot & Cucumber
In a pot, bring 1 Tbsp red wine vinegar, 1 tsp sugar, 1 tsp salt, and 2 Tbsp water to a boil. Turn off heat. Add 1 sliced shallot; let stand 12 minutes, then drain. Top 16 toasted baguette slices with 4 ounces Boursin cheese, sliced cucumber, and pickled shallots.

4. Mango & Pepper Jelly
Mix ½ chopped mango, ⅓ cup pepper jelly, 1 tsp lime zest, and 1 tsp lime juice. Top 16 toasted baguette slices with 4 ounces goat cheese and the mango-pepper jelly mixture.

5. Pimiento Cheese & Bacon
Mix 8 ounces grated cheddar cheese, ¼ cup mayonnaise, a 4-ounce jar diced pimientos, 1 tsp Dijon mustard, and ⅛ tsp cayenne. Top 16 toasted baguette slices with the cheese mixture, 4 slices broken cooked bacon, and sliced pickled okra.

6. Smoked Trout & Apple
Top 16 toasted baguette slices with ½ cup crème fraîche, ¼ cup sliced apple, 8 ounces flaked smoked trout, and 2 Tbsp dill.

7. Blue Cheese & Date
Top 16 baguette slices with 6 ounces blue cheese and 8 chopped pitted dates. Broil until melted. Top with honey.

8. Spicy Pea & Feta
Mash 2 cups cooked peas, 4 tsp olive oil, 1 Tbsp grated lemon zest, and salt. Place on 16 toasted baguette slices. Top with 4 ounces feta and pepper flakes.

9. Miso Butter & Radish
Mix 4 Tbsp butter and 1 Tbsp miso. Top 16 toasted baguette slices with the miso butter, 6 sliced radishes, 1 sliced scallion, and toasted sesame seeds.

10. Avocado & Olive
Mash 1 avocado and salt; place on 16 toasted baguette slices. Top with ⅓ cup sliced olives, sambal, and lemon zest.

11. Artichoke & Gruyère
Combine 4 ounces cream cheese, 2 ounces grated Gruyère, 2 Tbsp minced red onion, and Kosher salt. Spread on 16 baguette slices. Broil until melted. Top with quartered artichoke hearts.

12. Prosciutto & Tomato
Top 16 toasted baguette slices with ½ cup mayonnaise, 16 sun-dried tomatoes, 4 ounces torn prosciutto, ½ cup arugula, and salt.

ALI FEDOTOWSKY-MANNO'S
PARTY POTATO CHIPS

These are the perfect treat to serve at holiday parties.

ACTIVE 10 minutes / **TOTAL** 15 minutes / **MAKES** 6 to 8 servings

INGREDIENTS

- 1 cup freshly grated Parmesan cheese
- 1½ Tbsp dried oregano
- 2 tsp smoked paprika
- 1 tsp yellow mustard powder
- 1 10-ounce bag kettle-cooked potato chips
- ¼ cup fresh parsley

INSTRUCTIONS

1 Heat the oven to 400°.

2 In a small bowl, toss the grated cheese with the oregano, paprika, and mustard until thoroughly combined.

3 Spread the potato chips out on a large baking sheet covered in tin foil. Try to keep the chips in a single layer, if possible.

4 Sprinkle ¾ cup of the cheese mixture over the chips.

5 Bake for 5 to 7 minutes, until cheese has melted and started to brown.

6 Remove from the oven; toss the remaining cheese mixture on top.

7 Garnish with fresh parsley. Serve warm or at room temperature.

CHRIS McNALLY'S
CLASSIC EGGNOG

“ My go-to recipe for casual holiday parties is a liquid one—I love making homemade eggnog. It's such a cozy, rich beverage and a cheery seasonal treat. Give it a try! **”**

ACTIVE 10 minutes / **TOTAL** 35 minutes, plus chilling / **MAKES** 16 cups or 32 servings

INGREDIENTS

- 12 large eggs
- 1¼ cups sugar
- ½ tsp salt
- 2 quarts whole milk
- 1 cup dark rum (optional)
- 2 Tbsp vanilla extract
- 1 tsp ground nutmeg, plus additional for sprinkling
- 1 cup heavy cream

INSTRUCTIONS

1 In 5-quart Dutch oven, with a wire whisk, beat the eggs, sugar, and salt until blended. Gradually stir in 1 quart milk and cook over low heat, stirring constantly, until the custard thickens and coats the back of a spoon well, about 25 minutes. Do not allow the mixture to boil or it will curdle. (Mixture should remain at about 160°F.)

2 Pour the custard into a large bowl; stir in the rum (if using), vanilla, ground nutmeg, and remaining 1 quart milk. Cover and refrigerate until well chilled, at least 3 hours.

3 In a small bowl, with a mixer on medium speed, beat the heavy cream until soft peaks form. With a wire whisk, gently fold the whipped cream into the custard mixture.

4 To serve, pour the eggnog into a chilled 5-quart punch bowl; sprinkle with nutmeg for garnish.

EIGHT FESTIVE COCKTAILS

Why not savor a special drink worthy of the season? Here's
how to mix up signature sips your guests will love.

1. Spicy Bloody Mary

Combine **46 ounces vegetable
juice**, **1 cup vodka**, **2 Tbsp
lemon juice**, **2 Tbsp chopped
dill**, **1 Tbsp horseradish**, **1 Tbsp
Worcestershire**, **1 Tbsp hot sauce**,
¾ tsp pepper, and **¾ tsp celery
seed**. Serve over **ice** with **dilly
beans**, **lemon wedges**, and **celery**.
MAKES 8

2. Rosemary-Grapefruit Fizz

Simmer **4 sprigs rosemary**, **½ cup
sugar**, and **½ cup water** until sugar
is dissolved; cool. Discard rosemary.
Mix rosemary syrup, **1 liter seltzer**,
3 cups grapefruit juice, **1½ cups
vodka**, and **dash of bitters**. Serve
over ice with **rosemary sprig**.
MAKES 8

3. Lambrusco Sangria

Combine **1½ cups pear nectar**,
¾ cup Grand Marnier, **1 cup halved
grapes**, **1 sliced pear**, and **1 sliced
lemon**; chill. Add a **750-milliliter
bottle Lambrusco wine**.
MAKES 8

4. Slow-Cooker Apple Cider

In a slow cooker, combine **64 ounces
apple cider**, **6 chai tea bags**,
2 cinnamon sticks, and **1 split vanilla
bean**. Cook on low 3 to 4 hours.
Discard the tea bags; stir in **¼ cup
lemon juice**. Serve warm with
apple slices and **cinnamon sticks**.
MAKES 8

5. Blood Orange Margarita

In a cocktail shaker, muddle
2 jalapeño slices and **3 sprigs
cilantro**. Add **1½ ounces tequila**,
½ ounce lime juice, and **ice**;
shake for 30 seconds. Serve
topped with **blood orange soda**,
jalapeño, and **cilantro**.
MAKES 1

6. Spiced Cranberry Punch

Combine **6 cups cranberry
juice cocktail**, **1½ cups spiced
rum**, **1½ cups orange juice**, and
¼ cup lime juice; chill. Serve with
cranberries.
MAKES 8

7. Bourbon Negroni

In a cocktail shaker, combine
1½ ounces bourbon, **¾ ounce sweet
vermouth**, **¾ ounce Campari**, and
ice; shake for 30 seconds. Serve
with an **orange peel**.
MAKES 1

8. Ginger & Apple Cooler

In a cocktail shaker, combine
2 Tbsp Calvados, **1 tsp maple
syrup**, **1 tsp lemon juice**, and
ice; shake for 30 seconds. Serve
topped with **wheat beer** or **ginger
beer** and **candied ginger**.
MAKES 1

ANSWER KEY FOR QUIZZES

CHAPTER 1

PAGES 24 & 25
Q: Can you ID the *Evergreen* films these scenes come from?

A: Top row, left to right:
Christmas in Evergreen;
*Christmas in Evergreen:
Letters to Santa*;
Christmas in Evergreen;
Christmas in Evergreen

Middle row, left to right:
*Christmas in Evergreen:
Letters to Santa*;
*Christmas in Evergreen:
Letters to Santa*;
Christmas in Evergreen

Bottom row, left to right:
*Christmas in Evergreen:
Tidings of Joy*;
*Christmas in Evergreen:
Tidings of Joy*;
*Christmas in Evergreen:
Tidings of Joy*;
*Christmas in Evergreen:
Tidings of Joy*

CHAPTER 2

PAGE 75
Q: Which photos are from films with Christmas in the title?

A: Top row, left:
Entertaining Christmas

Middle row, left:
Christmas Everlasting

Middle row, right:
Christmas in Evergreen

Bottom row, right:
A Song for Christmas

CHAPTER 3

PAGES 138 & 139
Q: ID the movie or show for each of these photos.

A: Top row, left to right:
Christmas Town;
A Veteran's Christmas;
A Dog Named Christmas;
Meet the Peetes

Middle row, left to right:
Engaging Father Christmas;
A Cheerful Christmas

Bottom row, left to right:
One Christmas Eve;
The Nine Lives of Christmas;
The Nine Lives of Christmas;
One Christmas Eve

CHAPTER 4

PAGES 160 & 161
Q: Can you ID the movies that feature these weddings?

A: Top row, left to right:
A Holiday Engagement;
A Bride for Christmas;
Marrying Father Christmas;
A Blue Ridge Mountain Christmas

Middle row, left to right:
Marry Us for Christmas;
Meet the Santas;
Merry Matrimony

Bottom row, left to right:
The Good Witch's Gift;
Christmas Bells Are Ringing;
Marry Me at Christmas;
A Blue Ridge Mountain Christmas

CHAPTER 4

PAGE 171
Q: Guess these Christmas movies and the actors and actresses who star in them.

A: Clockwise from top left:
Memories of Christmas;
A Christmas Melody;
Christmas at Dollywood;
Christmas Getaway;
Christmas in Evergreen: Tidings of Joy;
A Godwink Christmas: Meant for Love

CHAPTER 5

PAGES 202 & 203
The Hallmark Movie Challenge
1) C, 2) A, 3) B, 4) A, 5) B, 6) C,
7) B, 8) B, 9) C, 10) A

Holiday Gift Guide

MAKE IT A HALLMARK CHRISTMAS

From keepsake ornaments to movie-watching must-haves, these festive finds are perfect for fans to give—and receive!

Rocking Horse Memories Keepsake Ornament
Hallmark.com / KeepsakeOrnaments

Hallmark Channel Movie Marathon Popcorn Bowl
Hallmark.com / ChristmasGifts

Hallmark Channel Movie Marathon Blanket
Hallmark.com / ChristmasGifts

Father Christmas Keepsake Ornament
Hallmark.com / KeepsakeOrnaments

***The Night Before Christmas* Pop-Up Book**
Hallmark.com / ChristmasGifts

INDEX

**HEARST
HOME**

Cover and book design by 10Ten Media

Library of Congress Cataloging-in-Publication Data is available.

10 9 8 7 6 5 4 3 2 1

Published by Hearst Home, an imprint of Hearst Home Books/Hearst Magazine Media, Inc.
300 West 57th Street, New York, NY 10019

For information about custom editions, special sales, premium and
corporate purchases: hearst.com/magazines/hearst-books

Printed in China

978-1-950785-24-7

Photo credits

Copyright Crown Media Family Networks 2020; Front Cover, 1, 5, 13, 15-27, 29-33, 35-37, 39, 40, 44, 57, 63, 65, 66, 69-72, 75-77, 79-83, 88, 89, 92, 105, 107, 108, 110, 111-115, 117, 128, 131, 132, 135-139, 141, 143, 144, 151, 153-156, 159-162, 164, 165, 167, 168, 171, 173, 174, 178, 185, 187, 193, 199, 202, 203, 205, 207, 213, 218, 219, 220, Back Cover 9dream studio 216; Brent Darby Photography LTD 145; Brett Stevens 209; Brian Woodcock 7, 59, 177, 179, 211, 217; bubble86 10, 11, 60, 61, 102, 104, 148, 149, 194, 195 various borders & trims; Burcu Avsar 97, 188, 189; Chris Cort 93; David Hillegas 101, 190; David Livingston 48, 124, 200, 208; David Tsay 65; Eivaisla 180; Elena Shashkina 49; FilippoBacci 56; Getty Inside Cover, 1, 2, 3, 224, pine, bows, trees, ornaments, trims and other various spot details; Ilya S. Savenok 212; Jennifer Gauld 123; LiliGraphie Front Cover, Back Cover; Manon Allard 5, 53; Marta Ortiz 175; Matt Winkelmeyer 202; maxsol7 46; Michael Partenio 98; Mike Garten 47,85; Miki Duisterhof 145; milanfoto 42; Miro Vrlik Photography 87; Nassima Rothacker 95, 145; NBCUniversal Media, LLC 90, 193; Nora Carol Photography 192; Paul Archuleta 84, 86, 118, 122, 126, 193, 197, 200, 202, 203, 206, 214; Pixelbliss 190; Rachel Whiting 146, 191; sergeykot 127; Shutterstock 52, 147, 201, pine, bows, trees, ornaments, trims and other various spot details; Stephanie Frey 91; StockphotoVideo 5, 129,183; Tuned_In 120; Ulyana Khorunzha 45; Vezzani Photography 125; Victoria Melnik 147; Viktory Panchenko 119; Virginia McDonald 51; Westend61 41; YelenaYemchuk 181; Yuki Sugiura 43; Yulia Naumenko 215; Yunhee Kim Front Cover, 121

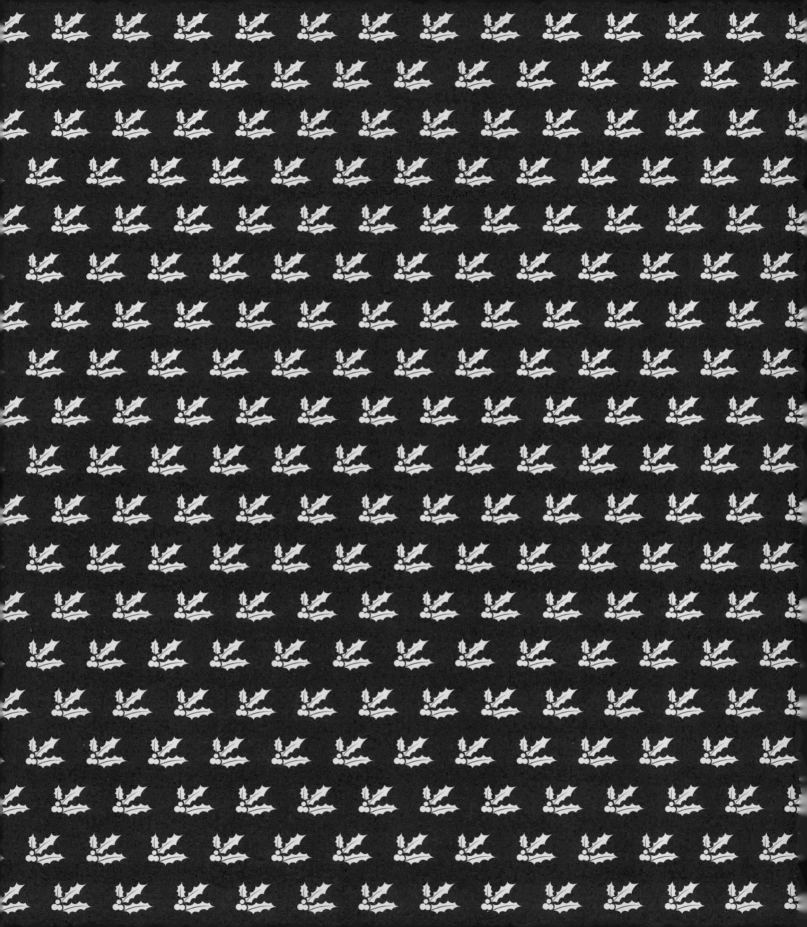